A LIFETIME OF DELTIC LOCOMOTIVES

Digital copy

Carstairs. With little day time work left in Scotland the locos would often visit this location. However the sight of 2 at the same time is somewhat rarer. 55018 and 55007 are seen with some more traditional WCML traction in May 79.

D9019 at Carlisle with the diverted Flying Scotsman On April 25th 1964. the train would have travelled via the Waverley Route crewed by a link 4 64B driver with a Gateshead crew taking charge at the Border City for the run over the Tyne Valley.

Chapter 1- Misspent youth

Chapter 2- My machine

Chapter 3- Deltic performance

Chapter 4- Deltics in Scotland

Chapter 5- Working with Deltics

Chapter 6- The final word

Introduction

The majestic Class 55 Deltic Locomotives have been a part of my life for just about as long as I can remember. As you will read in this book it's a love affair that's waxed and waned but never really ended.

The motivation to write came about whilst recovering from major surgery over the winter of 2016 and with so many memories and photographs along with a large circle of friends and former colleagues who worked on the class in British Railways service it seemed at the time important for me to get my story written down for posterity. Now those same friends and colleagues have inspired me to do a revised version of the book and to add in some new material for good measure.

So come with me on a trip down memory lane and enjoy reading about 22 exquisite locomotives doing the job for which they were built day in and day out along the ECML.

All images are from my own private collection and therefore my copyright unless otherwise shown.

With thanks

This book is dedicated to the memory of my late Grandfather Alfred Davies for it was he who introduced to the Deltics in 1969 and ensured I had my regular fix of mother Napier in my formative years.

This book would not have been possible without the help of friends old and new. It therefore gives me great pleasure to convey my thanks to the following people.

- Pete Chambers- My oldest friend from back in those wonderful days.
- Paul Nash- A new friend who once again provided some pure nostalgia.
- Gary Cannell - A new friend who once again provided some pure nostalgia.
- Alistair Smith – My old boss and a former Gateshead Deltic man.
- Richard Brown- York second man and ace photographer.
- The late Bob Peach - An old basher and contributor of material for this book.
- Paul Gildersleve- An old friend from the glory days and Deltic logger supreme.
- Matt Stodden- Waverley Route expert.
- Chronicles of Napier website- The go to place for all things Deltic.
- Harry Archibald- A man who has been there and is wise beyond words.

- My wife Jane for putting up with me as I spend hours writing away.

How things used to be 1- A busy early 1970's scene taken from platform 8 at the Cross.

How things used to be 2- A Harry Archibald late 1960's classic at east side of Kings Cross. Copyright Harry Archibald

Chapter 1

Misspent Youth

My first encounter with a Deltic locomotive took place at York in the summer of 1969 (my own summer of love as opposed to the real one a couple of years earlier led by the Hippie movement in the USA). My grandfather and I were on a day trip together to visit many of the fabulous museums in York. Not long after arriving into one of the bay platforms, from Leeds on a smoking old Metro Cammell 3 car unit, **MELD** grumbled to a halt in the old platform 14 with a Newcastle bound service. I was captivated by this huge noisy monster with the short shining nameplate and so began a love affair that's waxed and waned but never really ended. Later the same day we saw **ARGYLL & SUTHERLAND HIGHLANDER** departing for the south, however by then we were out on the city walls so it was not quite as intense an experience as number 3 had provided, and of course the first impression was already made a few hours earlier. However I must add the size of 21's nameplate along with that large and intricate crest has stayed with me and without doubt led to me always leaning towards having a preference to Scottish Deltics going forwards.

From then onwards, the locomotives came into my life on a fairly regular basis with trips to Leeds, Doncaster, Newcastle and Scotland. My first recorded haulage was behind **ROYAL HIGHLAND FUSILIER** on a totally full and standing southbound *Aberdonian* on March 29th 1974 on the outward leg of a family holiday to Yorkshire. Growing into my teens this love affair grew in intensity as I became more independent along with having money and the ability to travel more to see and photograph Deltics at work. By the time I was 14 years of age all Deltics had been seen on numerous occasions including both **NIMBUS** and **ROYAL SCOTS GREY** in Halifax after working the cotton town's portion of the 1730 ex Kings Cross. Most of the class had also been captured hard at work on the ECML, particularly around York and Darlington. Haulage however was still a different matter and at the time I could only claim haulage from a handful of locomotives including thankfully the soon to be side-lined **ST PADDY**. Family holidays to/from Yorkshire afforded numerous trips on the southbound *Aberdonian* and northbound *North Britain*. The former was an almost solid 55 turn with the Leeds always producing nothing better than a Holbeck chuck out class 47. Sadly my first trip to London Kings Cross in the school holidays in August 1977 also produced 47's both ways on the 1054 from Darlington and 1500 return a few days later, an early introduction to being bowled out by these hideous contraptions. However my interest in the southern end of the ECML was well and truly formed, on the trip we saw numerous 55's up close at Kings Cross including 55003/55020 and 55022.

1978: saw my real introduction to the bashing scene and the start of my quest to building up some significant mileages behind each locomotive. This was of course the era of punk rock, the continued dominance of Liverpool FC and one of the last years of full employment before Thatcher came to power and changed everything. Argentina had won their own world cup earlier that summer by defeating the Netherlands 3-1 in Buenos Aires with the flamboyant Mario Kempes scoring twice for the hosts in a thrilling match. The less said the better about the contribution of Scotland and Ally MacLeod and his world beating team to the tournament, although the song 'don't cry for me Argentina' seemed entirely appropriate. Grease the teen love story starring John Travolta and Olivia Newton John, with its cliques and peer pressure was the must see movie of the summer. Although despite seeing the film at least twice, much of my own summer was of course spent in pursuit of the 'twenty two'. The purchasing of a stopwatch and a half decent camera allowed a first attempt at logging the final months of the heavy Anglo Scottish and fast West Riding services along with some better photographs predominantly at Kings Cross and Peterborough. In fact my first logged run was behind **TULYAR** on the 0900 to Edinburgh on July 13th 1978 and resulted in some fast 110mph running with the care worn Finsbury Park thoroughbred.

55016 gets a wash and brush up at its home depot of Haymarket on 11/4/77. The loco left the shed soon after as 0E11 for the Waverley.

55005 departs from Darlington with an Edinburgh service on 31/5/80

My main travelling companion during this period was the long-time DPS member and bloody nice bloke Pete Chambers from Liverpool, someone who thanks to the power of the internet I have recently been reunited with after a gap of over 35 years. Towards the end of 1978 my Christmas holidays were spent admiring Deltics at Kings Cross or travelling between London and Peterborough/Doncaster. The highlight of which was trips behind 55003/6/14/15 and a close encounter with **GORDON HIGHLANDER** on its most welcome but very short lived escape from Doncaster Works.

As 1979 dawned my last full term at school got underway before leaving for good after the exams in May. The Pittsburgh Steelers were crowned Super Bowl champions after beating the almost invincible Dallas Cowboys 35-31 in Miami, Sex Pistols lead Sid Vicious died from an overdose and a little known trouser arousing actress called Catherine Bach was about to burst onto our screens playing good ole 'Daisy Duke' in the hit American TV show 'The Dukes of Hazard'. The year would go onto give us the McDonalds 'Happy Meal' and not much else other than of course one Margret Hilda Thatcher and the end of society as we knew it. Clowns to the left of me jokers to the right as the song goes!

Back on the rails, April saw another ECML jaunt and the start of a lifelong friendship with another Deltic man from London area the much respected and well liked Paul Gildersleve. During the course of a week's rover we enjoyed significant mileage behind 55002/3/5/7/11/13/18/19 and 22. The bash included **BALLYMOSS** on the rampage with the 1500 out of the Cross non-stop to York, and also a rancid trip to Hull on the 0356 from Doncaster behind **MELD** shortly after the locomotive had received the white cab treatment. Unfortunately for me, my bashing really got going at the time of the chronic and often critical power unit shortages. It was not uncommon for locomotives to languish in works for weeks, months and years waiting power units to become available. Often the ECML would only have a handful of machines in traffic as train after train ran late due to inferior motive power just not being able to keep time. Class 31's, 40's and 46's were all pressed into front line service to help fill the gap. I even remember 1E35 arriving in Doncaster with a March steam heat class 37 at its head one night. As the train was booked Doncaster drivers the 37 went through to the Cross but stupidly I didn't and waited for the next Deltic service hauled by 55009. Even though the novelty of a 37 into London was high.

The high summer months were spent growing my hair 1970's style along with undertaking casual labour on the new A9 road upgrade in the Highlands, and building up my Deltic mileage in between. Unlike the previous summer it was south of York and overnights only, as the closure of the route between Berwick and Dunbar following the Penmanshiel tunnel collapse in March really restricted the moves available during daylight hours.

On Monday 4th February 1980 my railway career begin and with access to privilege travel my status as a credible mileage man was finally established. Despite living on the Black Isle it was still possible to spend time on the ECML on at least a couple of full weekends per month and this boosted with 5 or 6 weeks rail roving during the course of the year led to my mileage on each locomotive passing the one thousand mark. My railway staff status also saw me have more ready access to driving cabs and footplate rides aboard **PINZA** and **TULYAR** were granted on services out of Edinburgh Waverley.

In many respects this year was the high water mark of my love affair with this iconic class, every spare moment was spent travelling or researching every aspect of Deltic operation. It became pretty obsessive stuff and the rest of my life was put on hold for the love of the remaining 20 locomotives. In fact on reflection, I am glad that I did not live on the ECML itself or I would have never gone home other than perhaps for an occasional bath. Despite my rural location such was my desperation that I averaged over 1200 miles per week behind Deltics during the course of the year. The following year 1981 continued as 1980 had ended, other than one by one each of our old friends fell by the wayside until by the time of my last serious Deltic based holiday only 15 of the class remained in traffic. For those of us who remember that last glorious summer it can never be said that the class went out with a whimper. Between May and the September, hardly a day went passed without a record of some kind being broken or an ever higher validated speed being recorded. For example, 120 mph running was achieved by 3 different locomotives (55008/16/19) on at least 5 occasions and just about every sectional running time on the stopping services were smashed as the curtain finally came down on this remarkable class. As the Deltic era ended the next high speed chapter began, namely the TGV one, with the first service running from Paris to Lyon on September 27th 1981 the circle of railway life turned another notch.

From 1982 until 1996 my interest in railways diminished to such an extent that in some years I could count my number of non-business related train trips on the fingers of one hand. The obsession from previous years had gone and now I was busy building a life and career for myself along with moving home several times as I moved up the greasy pole of corporate life. Any cranking journeys that I did make were more often than not wholly within Scotland and never involved overnights or any significant festering.

By 1996 we began to hear rumours of something which a few years earlier had seemed totally impossible and that was a return to mainline running for **ROYAL SCOTS GREY**. As the year unfolded the rumour seemed to be gathering momentum and when 55022 entered Springburn for its mainline overhaul, we all knew the dream was about to become reality. The date of the return was set for November 30th 1996 and I arrived in Edinburgh on a class 91 hauled service long before the *Deltic Deliverance* carriages had arrived from the south. I walked round to Market Street above Waverley station; this was the location that the locomotive for many of our back in the day south bound overnights would be first seen after leaving one of the well-known public houses up on the Royal Mile. Before long the air was filled with something not heard in the city for 15 years and that was of course the sound of a Deltic running light engine through the station in readiness for a southbound departure and didn't it sound grand as the damp November air was charged with the spine tingling mumble of D9000. I won't however dwell on the Berwick Barbeque as unless you've been in outer space for almost 20 years it's well known and much documented.

The superb 55005 is seen running out of Kings Cross for servicing after arriving up road with 1E05. The clue as to what it worked north is there for all to see.

My only lasting criticism of the day is many of the original shareholders were forgotten about or so it seemed anyway by the new brooms running the D9000 fund.

Suffice to say I went on to enjoy numerous mainline trips with RSG over the following years including an authorised cab ride on the WCML in March of 1997. A favour called in with an old work colleague getting me that all important cab guest invitation. It was at this time I first met Chris Wayman, a man who I would get to know well and grow to have a huge amount of respect and admiration for on the VXC adventures which lay ahead. So let's take a trip down memory lane and back to 1978 and a world very different from today.

55015 TULYAR is seen at Newcastle after arriving with 1E29 from Edinburgh in February 1980.

55018 BALLYMOSS and 55015 TULYAR are seen in Newcastle during the early hours of 28/1/80

The Bashing Years

Forever Autumn-1978

My first solo adventure began on Saturday 15th October with an up road *Clansman* run all the way from Inverness to Euston. I can't for the life in me remember what I did on the Sunday but it was away from the ECML and probably involved 50's out of Paddington or 45's on the Midland Region. As a 15 year old the rules set by my parents were no overnights and home to my Aunts in Epsom by 9.30pm, not unreasonable and a fair price to pay for a week long ticket. On Monday 16th, I was up bright and early and arrived into Waterloo via Wimbledon as opposed to the longer route via Sutton which I had taken the previous day. It was quickly down onto the underground, destination Kings Cross. One of the great pleasures in life for a teenager involved rushing up from the tube at Kings Cross to see what 55's if any sat on the blocks. This activity in my life coincided with the release of the superb Jam song 'down in a tube station at midnight'. A tune which along with 'nights in white satin' (or nights with the white cabs as it would later be renamed by us) sung by the Moody Blues would become bashing anthems and night time favourites on the juke boxes in various buffets up/down the line. However I digress, after finding your departure platform next came the joy of hopefully seeing the twin plumes of exhaust climbing steadily into the sky at the head of your train as you walked down the passed the long rake of coaching stock desperately scanning for any clues to the identity of the machine which would imminently be whisking you northwards. Back to the16th and I was ecstatic to find the Haymarket legend 55013 **THE BLACK WATCH** at the head of the 0900 hours so it was right away York. 13 would be heading home to Scotland calling at Peterborough, York, Darlington and Newcastle along the way. The opportunity of being let loose on the Southern half of the line was so enticing that anything north of York at this stage didn't even enter my mind. Despite having an additional 10 minutes padding in its schedule for single line working through Peascliffe tunnel in connection with engineering works to clear the line for 8ft 6ins container trains, 1S17 was a solid connection into the 0900 up from Edinburgh at York. The fester was short and not long after the northbound departure of 13 the bright yellow snout rounded the curve past the TMD to confirm 1E05 had produced its booked power as 55019 rolled majestically past and to a halt in platform 5. My day had got off to a dream start, Haymarket down road for another Haymarket machine up road. Little did I know however but my dream was soon to become a living nightmare. As RHF hammered its 11 coach train back to London it began to dawn on me that all wasn't well on the ECML. Train after train we had passed during the course of the morning ran late and mostly a 47 vice 55. Its only when I arrived in London did I realise how bad things actually were. I wandered aimlessly around for the rest of the day and even did a Peak to Leicester and back such was the sad state of affairs as each and every KX departure failed to produce anything better than a class 47. I consoled myself with a 12p coffee to wash down the 24p Lyons fruit pie purchased from the Buffet car as a 45/1 stormed my train north through the Bedfordshire countryside. This really wasn't how things should be panning out and it was with a heavy heart I made my way back through Suburbia to Epsom and bed. The following morning saw me make the same move for 1S17 only to find one big strumming 47 at the head of the 11 coach rake. The 0904 Leeds was also a 47 so I had no choice other than to suffer a 47 to Doncaster and see if any Deltics may be coming up road from Leeds or further afield. Following a brew and some people watching in the superbly named *St Ledger* buffet, normal service was resumed to some degree with a grubby but high performing 55005 on 1A15 the 1020 ex Newcastle. After finding a seat in the rear coach, it was right away London calling at Peterborough only. Once again I must have suffered a 47 down road as my next encounter with a legend was with the equally grubby 55002 on 1E14 the up *Aberdonian*. Number 2 managed to work this train for 4 consecutive days 16th-19th and was very much flying the flag for absent classmates. Another short digression is in order at this point as it's probably worth sharing the weekly availability position. The headlines showed 14 locomotives out of traffic with 13 in works and 1 stopped at depot. In respect of the locomotives in works, 19 overhauled power units would have been needed to get them all back into traffic, With only 2 overhauled units on the shop floor and a further 10 forecast to be ready by year end it was never going to happen.

Therefore as history now shows, locomotives stood idle as good power units were robbed from one Deltic to get another back into traffic. This period was of course the beginning of the end for 55001/20 and also saw the long term storage of 55004. To be frank, things would never be the same again but little did we know it at the time. During the course of my rover, the above situation left 8 locomotives for 12 diagrams without taking daily maintenance exams and fuelling into consideration.

Locomotive	Location	Reason
55001	Doncaster Works	Waiting power units
55003	Doncaster Works	On works since 17/8 waiting power units
55004	Doncaster Works	Waiting power units
55007	Doncaster Works	On works since 18/7 having its final intermediate repair
55009	Doncaster Works	Waiting power units
55010	Doncaster Works	Classified light repair
55012	Haymarket/Finsbury Park	Numerous defects
55014	Doncaster Works	Unclassified repair
55015	Doncaster Works	Power unit change, released 19/10
55016	Doncaster Works	Waiting power units
55018	Doncaster Works	Power unit change, released 25/10
55020	Doncaster Works	Waiting power units
55021	Doncaster Works	Waiting power units
55022	Doncaster Works	Power unit change, released 25/10

After another long fester about Kings Cross, along with all of its interesting comings and goings plus of course the darker side of society who dossed down in the numerous empty warehouses and buildings nearby and would often come onto the station to beg or in some cases steal whatever they could before once again being ejected out into the night. 55017 produced for the 2230 to Edinburgh diverted via the Joint Line due to planned overnight closures between Grantham and Newark presenting me with an opportunity for 393+ miles of solid overnight and a choice of either 1E01 or 1E05 back south.

Sadly and not unsurprisingly, **THE DURHAM LIGHT INFANTRY** was removed from the train at Newcastle with a mechanical defect and retreated to its home depot for repairs. This left me in a flap as I didn't want to go blind to Edinburgh nor did I want another 125 miles of steam heat 47 in my book. Therefore after alighting from my warm compartment, I decided to see if any of the following overnights would produce which of course they didn't, with both 12 and 16 wheel junk bowling me out badly.

So all that was left was a class 45/0 on the 0800 departure to Bristol to see what if anything was about in York, however, both the short and long answer was the same 'Nothing'.

After a breakfast in town, I went back to the station to wait for 1E01 the 0705 ex Edinburgh to arrive at 1018 and the short 32 minute trip to Doncaster. At the time **THE BLACK WATCH** was my highest mileage Deltic so I didn't want to go right through to London on 1E01 and with hindsight I'm glad that I didn't. After a short wait, **THE GREEN HOWARDS** was taken back to York on the 1100 departure to Edinburgh. Special stop at Doncaster for reasons unknown.

1S17 was standing room only so it was the front vestibule right behind 55008 for me for the nonstop run to York. As we arrived in platform 14, I saw 55011 arriving into platform 8 with the 1139 arrival ex Newcastle. I flew over the footbridge as only a 16 year old can and dived aboard the London train just as the departure bell was ringing to get 1A15 rolling. A second trip to Doncaster was had this time with 55011 and another impressive (not) 32 miles in the book. What my motive was I have no idea, however, with a huge amount of luck, and totally blind I fell onto 55006 hauling the 1246 departure to Harrogate. Therefore by default my one and only Class 55 hauled trip to Harrogate went into the book. With my nerves in tatters and all my luck long since used up, I took 55006 all the way back to Kings Cross with the return working at 1652 and so ended another eventful day.

The penultimate day of my rover saw the booked Epsom to Kings Cross move for 1S17 and a trip to York with the ever reliable 55019 **ROYAL HIGHLAND FUSILIER** on a customary very well filled train. My heart was in my mouth as I waited to see if the southbound 1216 departure would produce for me again. I must say I was surprised to see 55006 at the head of the train as I had last saw the old girl in London the previous evening at 2030 or so. However, any Deltic was a welcome one and Kings Cross was by now the only logical destination. After arriving back at Kings Cross I had a walk over to St Pancras to view proceedings before heading back to the Cross. Walking back at the station I was hugely delighted by the site of **THE BLACK WATCH** at the country end of the 1608 to York a service not booked to be hauled by a Deltic at this time (The loco would later work to Stockport on the mail after arriving in York) I already knew the afternoon Leeds had been a Deltic so the 20 minute wait at Doncaster was stress free. Gateshead provided the power and number 8 for my final southbound trip and an on time arrival In London brought the curtain down on my last full day. After wishing Pete Chambers all the best it was a leisurely trip to Epsom by way of my usual tube leap and a platform 2 suburban side departure from Waterloo out over the wonderfully named 'music hall and necropolis' viaducts towards Clapham Junction and bed.

The morning of Friday October 20th dawned in suburbia with a bright and fiery autumnal sunrise helping to usher in a sunny day and more falling leaves. After saying my goodbyes to my relatives, I was ready for the final 4-SUB commute into Waterloo on the 0757 all stations via Wimbledon and a rush hour trip across town for 1S17. Although on this occasion with added pressure of knowing I had to take the train regardless of power. The 09:00 was booked off platform 4 and it was immediately clear as I came up from the tube that the twin plumes were once again in evidence-My Lords! The week was going to end on an end to end maximum mileage move. Gateshead depots hugely grimy 55005 **THE PRINCE OF WALES'S OWN REGIMENT OF YORKSHIRE** was the allocated locomotive and put in its usual high quality performance. Even a good 10 minutes before departure, the train was wedged as usual; thankfully however, I got an outside seat in a front coach bay of 4 thus avoiding the need to stand for the first 2 hours at least. Time to relax as barring any failure; it was next stop Edinburgh or Heading-Bra as the lady station announcer at York appeared to call the Scottish capital.

We arrived right time into the Waverley at 1446 and job done for me at least. Engine for the shed I overheard the shunter tell the signaller via the signal post telephone and with a baleful honk on the horn 55005 blasted out of the station for Haymarket TMD and servicing.

After working up from Yorkshire with the Leeds Executive on 28/10/77 number 9 sits on the Blocks at Kings Cross.

55012 CREPELLO arrives in Selby with a York service on 15/4/79

55009 ALYCIDON cruises through County Durham in August 1978 whilst working up to London.

Forever Autumn-1979

The story begins at Kings Cross on Sunday 16th of September 1979. Most of the day had been wasted chasing 55010 **THE KINGS OWN SCOTTISH BORDERER** and getting bowled by numerous 47's. However after much flapping, I finally arrived at Kings Cross on time behind 55017 **THE DURHAM LIGHT INFANTRY** on the 1910 from York so this at least ensured that I had the pick of the numerous overnight trains.

My own favourite train was the 2240 to Edinburgh and with several Deltics in position to work north, things looked good. Sure enough 55006 **THE FIFE & FORFAR YEOMANRY** did the honours and with so many 55's apparently heading to Scotland, Edinburgh seemed the logical destination. For me personally 55006 never underperformed and she went like hell in the night with her well filled train, all was well in my world.

As the saying goes after the show comes the fall, Edinburgh Waverley just after 0600 on a damp Monday morning. The options open to me were limited to, the dreaded fester in those funny little red plastic chairs outside the travel centre and a wait to see if the 0725 to Newcastle produces a Deltic, or a quick spin to Glasgow and back for the 0950 to Plymouth?. I hated 1E08, due mainly to the rancid stock, it tottered along at 60-80mph and upon arrival Newcastle you had no obvious next move to make. I decided on Glasgow, a ubiquitous class 47/7 each way filled the best part of 2 hours and offered some warmth and doss time despite the dentist chair like seating. Passing Haymarket I saw 55006 in the fuel bay and also more surprisingly the black headcode of a mystery Deltic in the shed (well not a mystery really with 55020 and 55022 in works it was Deltic 8) **THE GREEN HOWARDS** had worked the down Plymouth into Edinburgh on the Sunday evening so in theory should have worked southbound overnight. I could only assume a defect of some description had prevented her doing so. Whatever it was must have been of a minor nature as 55008 later produced for 1V93 and gave a good account of herself on the big train.

With so many machines still in Scotland, the obvious move was 1V93/1S27 and then a southbound overnight. However, plans quickly changed upon arriving in York, passing the depot I noticed 55010 coming off shed to work the 1410 York to Kings Cross, So it was farewell to **THE GREEN HOWARDS** and hello my machine. However, every silver lining has its cloud, which in the case of 1A22 was the amount of slow running it did. I even believe it was booked slow line from Peterborough to St Neots to allow shiny but more often than not late running HST services to overtake. The 'stagger', added to the fact many York drivers had a reputation of never going above 98 mph, made it a train to avoid unless needed to get you in position for down evening departures from London. Today was no exception and I decided to leap from 55010 at Huntingdon and leave fellow basher Richard Campbell who was off to work dossing to the Cross with my machine.

After a short wait, and not for the last time that week I fell onto 55011 **THE ROYAL NORTHUMBERLAND FUSILIERS** at Huntingdon on a northbound train, on this occasion on the 1649 to York .After the bad experiences of leaping at Grantham and Newark for endless class 47 hauled services the previous day still fresh in my mind, I decided to stick with Number 11 to York and back to London on 1A34 due into Kings Cross at 2302. A sound high mileage move other than if it was more than a few minutes late you would miss 1L22 at 2300 and 1S79 at 2315, thus leaving yourself with a very limited amount of overnights to choose from. That is exactly what happened, as we came out of Gasworks and across the throat, 55009 **ALYCIDON** was leaving on 1L22 for Bradford.

A huge fester within the less than salubrious confines of Kings Cross now took place as everything strummed or whistled right up to my last possible train out of London at 0110. 1L00 was predominantly a Newspaper and mail train with limited seating but still a useful train for those who needed it. Can you even begin to imagine the state I had got myself into as I stood on the end of platform 8 waiting the locomotives arrival from Finsbury Park depot?

My relief was immense as an immaculate 55015 **TULYAR** backed down onto the train. After leaping aboard, it was to find the train already wedged with an eclectic mix of humainity. It was carnage, with at least half a dozen people to every compartment, and many others standing or sitting in the vestibules. This was after all a popular train with party animals heading north after a night out in the capital or those returning from holiday via Gatwick airport in the days before regional airports became so popular.

My partying was of a slightly different kind as **TULYAR** erupted in the dip at the bottom of Gasworks Tunnel and the train filled with white exhaust as we powered effortlessly through the London suburbs and out into the sticks. Thankfully, the L00 gradually emptied on the journey north, although minimum doss was always guaranteed on this train. The first rays of another sunny morning saw us arriving in Leeds just before 0530. 55015, was off to York and her next working the 0805 to Kings Cross and I was off to Selby for a different 00 this time 1A00 the 0606 from York. The 'Fart Cart' working the 0538 to Hull deposited me at Selby on time at 0612 to wait the arrival of one of my most favourite early morning trains. The handful of restless passengers picked up their belongings as the twin Napier's of 55008 **THE GREEN HOWARDS** heralded the arrival of this superb train. I was beginning to wonder if the loco had a non-operational boiler as she had clearly worked 1S27/1E26 since we parted company at York the day before.

Once again Huntingdon seemed the obvious leaping point, this time for 1D00 the 0852 all shacks to Hull. After trips on IL00/1A00 and now 1D00, it was more than a case of déjà vu as 55011 again did the honours on a down departure from Huntingdon. Number 11 seemed to like working to Hull during the latter days of its career as someone nicknamed it **THE ROYAL NORTHUMBERSIDE FUSILIERS** such was the locomotives appetite for the Hull road.

When on a Hull service, I always looked out to see how the new Humber Bridge was progressing. This impressive 2km long single span bridge from Barton on Humber to Hessle, was a magnificent construction project, although I am unsure what benefits it actually brought to the area. The bridge finally opened in June 1981 and its completion therefore took place shortly after the day time Class 55 era to Hull had ended. My last ever Deltic on this route in daylight hours was behind 55010 on March 15th almost 3 months before the bridge saw its first road vehicles. After the usual lunchtime fester around the station it was another dose of 55011 back to London on 1A18. At least this train had a bit of variety, as it ran nonstop from Doncaster to Peterborough with an arrival time at the Cross of around 1545.

55017 **THE DURHAM LIGHT INFANTRY** was rejected on the 1605 to York, as the Loco for 1D04 the down *Hull Executive* was none other than 55010. Having your favourite Deltic on this prestigious business service nonstop to Retford was just about the best ticket in town and tonight was no exception. Lots of 106-108 mph running and a credible 100 minute 35 seconds to Retford despite a string of slacks, signal checks and a trip up Stoke bank on the slow line, for no obvious reason other than to clear the rust off the rails.

At Retford, I left number 10 to continue north to Hull and I headed south again with another former Haymarket stalwart 55019 **ROYAL HIGHLAND FUSILIER** on 1A31, the 1811 York to Kings Cross and another Hellfire run with a Kings Cross driver going home. Number 19 was driven hard to ensure an on time arrival in London.

This once again gave me the pick of the overnights and a possible night with the white cabs, 55007 **PINZA** on 1S70 and 55003 **MELD** on 1S72. In a moment of utter madness, **MELD** was only taken to Peterborough for 55006 **THE FIFE & FORFAR YEOMANRY** to Doncaster on the following 1L22 Bradford service. Thankfully the wait at Doncaster was a short one with 55005 taking me back to London on the 0212 departure. I was asleep by Rossington and remember nothing further until peering out of the window at a cold grey platform 6 at Kings Cross.

White cabs were back on the agenda again as 55015 **TULYAR** worked the first down departure at 0550, therefore after running the gauntlet of the unsavoury night life in the station area we were soon on our way northwards once again. More dossing was in order in the warm and quiet mark 2d coach. Although I must have been awake at Peterborough as I saw 55010 on the stock of the 0750 commuter train to London. This made me reflect on a possible move later in the day; KOSB should now be well placed for a lunchtime trip to Hull or York and then an overnight to Scotland later on. After weighing things up for all of 10 seconds, I decided to get off 1S12 at Doncaster, to head south this time on 1A08 which gave me a surprise with 55007 **PINZA** at the helm as I'd last seen her at Kings Cross on 1S70 a few hours earlier. Any basher with a sleeper berth must have been well and truly bowled!!

Back at the Cross my eyes were aimed at the direction of Gasworks, and the appearance of the locomotives for the 1205 to Hull and 1220 to York. A Class 47 slithered out of the tunnel for 1D02 and now what was left of my reputation was on 1L42 producing. Thankfully, a large yellow snout emerged from the gloom. However, it was immediately obvious that it was not 55010. A further dose of 55011 was in store instead. However, with not much sleep the night before I decided to stick to plan and take RNF to York and back to have a more restful afternoon. Whilst this R&R was underway, 55013 **THE BLACK WATCH** worked the 1305 to Cleethorpes. A 47 on a Deltic diagram to Hull and a Deltic on a 47 diagram to Cleethorpes, confused? I was. If it wasn't for bad luck I'd have no luck at all.

Arriving back in London at around 19:00, I booked into a doss parlour over the road from the Cross to have a good night's rest and to start again refreshed the next day. The hotel was still there in 2012 although disused but visible on my daily commute on the 205 bus from Marylebone to Old Street; from the upper deck of the bus I passed at eye level the window of the room purchased for £8 including breakfast way back then. After breakfast, it was a short walk to the KX all ready for another stint on the road. Finsbury Park kindly chucked out 55009 **ALYCIDON** just for me on the 0805 to Hull. I had the whole of the front coach to myself on this sociable train. As we blasted out of the Cross I spied 55019 **ROYAL HIGHLAND FUSILIER** backing down onto a set of Mk 1 coaches in platform 7, which would of course form the 0838 to York as booked off the 0630 ex Peterborough. I rather fancied a trip in a mark one compartment and therefore number 9 was only taken to Peterborough, to enable me to have a day time overnight with number 19.1L40 really was an enigma it's stopping pattern was Peterborough and then York, a very fast, semi fast?

This led to a most enjoyable trip to York and back to Doncaster in the company of 55019, before meeting up with 55009 for a trip to our capital city on the return working from Hull. The novelty in those days of a Peterborough and Kings Cross only trip with a Deltic was almost too good to miss. Back in the smoke and 55014 The **DUKE OF WELLINGTONS REGIMENT** produced for the 1605 to York. My favourite ex Gateshead machine had worked up to London earlier in the day after coming off a 'C' exam at York so it was a most pleasant surprise to see her. A good dose of The Duke was had to Doncaster and I would almost certainly have had her through to York and back on 1A34 1956 York to King's Cross if it was not for the fact 55010 **THE KINGS OWN SCOTTISH BORDERER** was working 1A31 1811 York to Kings Cross.

Several of us sat in the Mark 1 catering vehicle and I vividly remember watching the china crockery vibrating like mad as No 10 romped down Stoke Bank at 112 mph and towards an on time arrival in London. I let both 55019 and 55021 go on northbound overnights, and had my second consecutive departure from the Cross with an ex Gateshead machine in the form of 55017 **THE DURHAM LIGHT INFANTRY** on 1L22 2300 to Leeds. It was on 1L22 that I bumped into my old Pete Chambers and we both undertook the 2am subway walk at Doncaster as we leapt from The D.L.I, onto 1E35 with 55007. A compartment was quickly found thanks to some train crew travelling passenger alighting at Doncaster. A solid night's Sleep (well 2.5 hours actually) saw another 4.30am arrival in London. We staggered to the front of the train just as number 7's power units were silenced, to be replaced by the sound of the Class 31 arriving with 5S12. A walk over to the all night KFC in the Euston Road for a coffee, and then it was back into the relative safety of Cubits magnificent terminal. On the way back to the station, a lady of the night offered to show me a good time for less than the price of a sleeper berth. I wonder if she knew that I had not had a wash for almost 24 hours or had a fresh change of clothes for a week.

Friday September 21st and the week was really beginning to take its toll now, it was all I could do to drag myself into the coaches for 1S12 and await the arrival of its locomotive. I soon awoke though as

55010 **THE KINGS OWN SCOTTISH BORDERER** backed down onto 1S12; I had scored again with my machine without even trying. Whilst I had been to Doncaster those nice men in Eastern Region control had kept Number 10 safe for me inside Finsbury Park and had even fitted some new brake blocks. Tempting as it was to go all the way with KOSB I left that to my travelling companion Pete Chambers and decided to try the novelty of a run on the up *Hull Executive*, 55009 **ALYCIDON** did the honours from Retford and whilst the run was nothing special I enjoyed the autumnal trip with the ageing racehorse.

Upon arrival in London I had to find a bank to top up my funds (no cash machines back then). Following a long layover and a visit to the famous and sadly now closed Kings Cross models, it was all aboard the 1205 to Hull and a dose of 55002 **THE KINGS OWN YORKSHIRE LIGHT INFANTRY**. I took KOYLI to Hull (just to check on Humber Bridge building progress) and back to Doncaster.

The 1829 to York arrived with 55006 at the helm and I decided to go all the way to York and back to London with this old warrior a good solid no nonsense move or so I thought.

This led to my first really massive bowl out of the week! By the time we arrived in London all available Deltics had worked north and all that was left for me was inferior motive power. I was a less than happy chap heading for Leeds on 1L00 that night, as it was the hiss of a class 47 which lulled me into a fitful sleep. I shared my compo with a family from Bradford who were returning from holiday in Spain with an oversized tourist tat toy donkey. I would dearly have loved a racehorse and not a donkey for company that night despite the presence of an extremely pretty and tanned toy donkey owning young lady.

Arriving in Leeds at 0530 it was time to say goodbye to my new found friends as they were off home in a taxi and could not believe that I was going to Selby only to go all the way back to London again, they thought I was mad but at least I didn't have sunburn and a straw donkey to show for my holidays. As I rattled my way out of Leeds on an eastbound unit I did not know that this cloud very much had a silver lining waiting for me.

The sun was still rising as I awaited the arrival of 1A00 at Selby, although for 1A00 the sun had almost set as this excellent early morning train to London entered its last few weeks of operation before being binned at the commencement of the winter timetable. My own farewell to the train could not have been better 55010 **THE KINGS OWN SCOTTISH BORDERER** did the honours and a most sociable trip was had to London in the company of Mr Moose and his son Mini-Moose. At the Cross the Donny lads went onto the tube and off to do something else and I headed back North almost straight away on the 1005 to York in the capable hands of 55019 **ROYAL HIGHLAND FUSILIER** .1D00 had strummed that morning and 55006 **FIFE & FORFAR YEOMANRY** had worked 1L40 so I decided to do 19 to Doncaster and 55006 to the Cross on 1A35 to cover 1L44 and 1D04. At Donny the gen was that 55022 **ROYAL SCOTS GREY** had worked the Doncaster works test train that morning after her final Intermediate repair and should with any luck be back gracing the ECML the following week. The other bit of platform end news was that 55005 **THE PRINCE OF WALES'S OWN REGIMENT OF YORKSHIRE** was coming light from York to re-engine 1A18. As there was no sign of POWORY by the time 55006 was ready to leave on 1A35 I decided to take No 6 to Peterborough and await the arrival of 1A18 there, thus if 55005 failed to produce I would still have 1L43 to fall back on. Plan B was however not needed as bang on time a very clean 55005 arrived drowning out the announcement of London Kings Cross only next train on Platform 3. The added bonus was that legendary Doncaster driver Joe Hodgson was in the chair of No 5 and would therefore be the driver of the down *Hull Executive* later that day.

55017 **THE DURHAM LIGHT INFANTRY** was rejected for the second time in a few days on the 1605 to York in favour of 55005 and Joe Hodgson on 1D04. As No 5 had only worked up from York there was no need to re-fuel her, and she was merely shunt released and placed at the head of 1D04 by a little after 1630 hrs. Little did I know it, but I was about to witness one of the all-time great runs on this short lived but famous train. 90 minutes 12 seconds to Retford with a maximum speed of 113mph certainly wasn't shabby. The rest of the day was somewhat over shadowed by this remarkable event but briefly comprised of 55013 **THE BLACK WATCH** back to London on 1A31, 55019 **ROYAL HIGHLAND FUSILIER** to Doncaster on 1L22 and 55012 **CREPELLO** back to Kings Cross on 1E35.

With only limited personal hygiene in the previous week and a bag of festering washing, it was time for a day off. I therefore had a one journey only restriction placed on me and a visit to my relative's house in Epsom was rostered by control.

After some much appreciated pampering, it was back on the iron road and for the second consecutive Sunday 1S72 produced for me and gave me a solid Scottish overnight. This time it was the turn of Finsbury Parks 55012 to do the honours. We left London in fine style, sadly somewhere north of Newcastle the gremlins struck and we began to lose time. When **CREPELLO** finally arrived in Edinburgh on only one engine the omens were not good for a totally successful second week.

In fact before the week was over, I was to become more of a class 47 basher than a Deltic basher. After the usual Monday morning spin to Glasgow and back, I once again enjoyed a former Gateshead Deltic on the 0950 Edinburgh to Plymouth train. This time 55005 **THE PRINCE OF WALES'S OWN REGIMENT OF YORKSHIRE** did the honours. The sensible, safe and maximum mileage move would have been a return to Edinburgh with The Prince; however this plan was soon kyboshed once I heard ultra low mileage 55003 was going to be the locomotive in charge of the 1550 to London. **MELD** looked glorious in the autumn sun shine and the plan was to ultimately catch up with number 3 for a second time later in the day on hopefully a northbound bound overnight. At the back of my mind was of course to write the wrongs of leaping from a trip to Edinburgh with Deltic 3 at Peterborough the previous week. The move that came together in my head at least was as follows, Take number 3 to Grantham; catch the 1605 ex London as far as Doncaster before finally heading up to London on 1A31 for the overnights.

The fester at Grantham was a long one, 1L44 was one duff and therefore I had well over a 2 hour wait before finally headed north behind 55015 **TULYAR** on the 1805 from Kings Cross. With the last up stopper a 47, no move was available other than right away to York behind number 15. A blind alley in many respects as you ended up in the middle of the ECML and in the wrong place for just about every possible move. I took myself off to the buffet to try and come up with a possible get out of jail move. Whilst festering over a tea along with looking at table 26 in the all line timetable, I could hear the unmistakable sound of an approaching Deltic. After gathering up my belongings and rushing outside, I was dismayed to find the Deltic had passed through the station and was now out under Holgate Bridge.

I had no sooner decided that my best move was to take the first HST to Newcastle in the hope that the 2025 ex Edinburgh would produce its booked Deltic power, when the droning of a 55 backing down onto the stock in platform 11, finally made me realise what was happening. The Deltic I had seen a few minutes earlier was actually the train engine for the 2208 passenger and postal service to Shrewsbury a train which tonight was to be hauled to Stockport by 55002 **THE KINGS OWN YORKSHIRE LIGHT INFANTRY** My bad luck of earlier had now put me in pole position for some rare Deltic track along with a trip over the Pennine hills. I bagged a few time exposure photographs including one with KOYLI standing next to the Peak hauled Newcastle-Bristol mails before finding an empty compartment for an overnight with a difference. After leaving Leeds sleep came easy and what seemed only a few minutes later, I awoke to see a Deltic standing on the opposite line outside my window. It took me a few minutes to work out what was going on. The Deltic was actually 55002 and we were in Stockport and unless extremely quick, I was about to be on an electric hauled train and quite possibly become the only person ever to have a Deltic on this train one way only. I gathered up my belongings and leapt out onto the platform just as the station supervisor was whistling up for 1M41 to depart next stop Crewe. After taking some time to calm down, it was time to admire this majestic Locomotive in such alien surroundings, although with no film left in my camera it was a memory only of KOYLI sitting in the middle road sparkling under the station lights. An uneventful return to York followed on the balancing train, before being deposited on a cold York station at around 0300. As I was walking over the footbridge four-seven something or other was arriving in platform 5 on one of the last southbound overnights. I wearily climbed aboard and was asleep within minutes.

Tuesday September 26th dawned cool and grey as the 47 slithered in Kings Cross in plenty of time for 1D00, the 0805 service to Hull. After a wash and brush up and some breakfast, I was pleased to see 55006 **THE FIFE & FORFAR YEOMANRY** was the allocated engine for the Hull train so it was an easy decision to make in terms of my ultimate destination, Hull and back would do nicely thank you. 3 hours of immense pleasure in the company of Deltic 6, a bit of Humber Bridge spotting an hour or so for lunch and a few photographs in the autumnal sun, and 3 hours back to Kings Cross set me up nicely for the down *Hull Executive* at 1705. Just as soon as I saw **THE KINGS OWN SCOTTISH BORDERER** back down onto the stock for 1D04 so a second trip to Hull in less than 12 hours was on the cards. Not the best decision in hindsight as I was taking myself up another blind alley without really thinking things through. However, it was 'Happy hour again and again' (apologies to Paul Heaton) The return working for 55010 was the 2100 Hull to Doncaster and then in theory onwards to Kings Cross on 1A41 after taking over from lesser power. In reality the engine would retire to Doncaster depot after working in from Hull and would come out for either the 0356 back to Hull or go light to York or London instead. So following another enjoyable trip to Hull, I found myself at Doncaster with no real options open to me. Unlike Monday night there was no Stockport move to get me out of trouble.

I took a 46 to Newark, for another back to Doncaster, a class 47 to Peterborough for 1L01 and its class 31 before ending up at Grantham in utter despair at dawn.

Rancid wasn't the word to describe this vile overnight. Thankfully my old friend 1A00 produced for me for one last time and I gratefully climbed aboard for the short trip to Peterborough behind 55019 and the hope of a Deltic to Hull on 1D00. This led to my third trip to Hull within 24 hours this time behind **CREPELLO** and my last ever trip with the locomotive before its windows had the white paint treatment the following month. Another rush of blood saw me alight from the return working at Peterborough and wait blindly for the 1405 ex Kings Cross to York, another hideous 47 made for a gloomy trip to Grantham. Normal service was resumed with a trip to Huntingdon with **MELD** on the 1410 from York, where I caught up with 55010 on the 1605 down (a train I could of course have boarded in London had I stuck with **CREPELLO** earlier on). Even now, I still wasn't done with bus stop bashing and I took my machine to Newark for 55019 **ROYAL HIGHLAND FUSILIER** on the 1810 ex York. After a couple of totally low quality overnights, it was time for a final night in a hotel before my final few days on the road and a WCML overnight home to Inverness.

After a shower and breakfast, I produced for the 1005 to York and some quality mileage behind 55021 **ARGYLL & SUTHERLAND HIGHLANDER**. York and back to Peterborough with the ASH set me up nicely for another York move this time with 55002 KOYLI on the 1605 from London, returning with the last up stopper at 1956 and an arrival in London at 2302. Sadly and perhaps not unsurprisingly the way the week was panning out another night devoid of any Deltic haulage was about to follow. My usual trains the 0005 to Newcastle and 1L00 both dropped and with no funds for a sleeper berth, all that was left was to take 1L00 to Peterborough, 1A40 to London and then suffer some class 31 action on the 0405 Kings Cross to Leeds. This left me with little sleep but nicely placed in Doncaster for the southbound 1A04 which thankfully was hauled by 55006. As we left Doncaster, I overheard some lads talking about some news they had been given earlier that ex works **ROYAL SCOTS GREY** was working the 0805 from York. After quizzing them further, I was sufficiently confident enough, that it was indeed true. I took the gamble and alighted from 1A04 at Retford to await events. I was hugely relieved with an immaculate RSG appeared in the distance as she took the 40mph turn out onto the platform line. The run up to London was uneventful, with a maximum speed of 101 mph and another competent performance from a locomotive which had been sorely missed in the previous few months. However, this was my last day and I needed to be back in London for the 2105 service from Euston to Inverness, so with this in mind, the moves today would need to be simple and low risk. Therefore my 14 day rover ended with a final bridge inspecting trip to Hull and back with 55006 **THE FIFE & FORFAR YEOMANRY** on the 1205 down and 1630 up line.

Chasing Deltics was very much a social thing, and rarely other than on some midweek daytime services would you not bump into someone you knew. However, when travelling alone there was always something of interest so let's take a look at a typical day time run from London to Doncaster.

After the excitement of 'blast off' had subsided and the Deltic had settled into the climb of Holloway bank, the next things to look out for would be Highbury stadium then home of Arsenal FC on the upside and of course Finsbury Park depot on the downside around four minutes into the journey. Necks would be stretched and strained to see what 55's if any happened to be about, and also for any racehorses hiding in the stable.

On the hill side once again on the downside was the Alexandra Palace or the 'Home of Darts' as it is now better known as. This iconic landmark was burned to the ground on July 10th 1980 and took many years to rebuild back to its former glory. I was on a rover on the night of the blaze, although much further north between York and Edinburgh when the actual fire took hold. So as the R&B singer Shaggy would go onto sing 20 years later "It wasn't me" Following extensive investigations, the cause of the blaze was eventually put down to an electrical fault.

After topping the climb out of London at Potters Bar, around 13 minutes out, our Deltic would usually hit 100mph for the first time as we roared through Hatfield just over 17 miles into the 156 mile journey, and a feel for what kind of man we had up front would begin to be formed depending on if the power was eased off or speed kept rising on the 1:200 descent.

More often than not, we would fly through the new town of Stevenage at 100mph as passengers on the narrow platforms took cover from the rampaging blue beast at the head of our train. I always felt Stevenage looked modern and futuristic, and perhaps what all towns would be like one day. Good transport interchange, shops, places to eat and a cinema all under one roof. As someone from the Highlands it really was impressive although perhaps those who lived there felt differently. However it was and continues to be is prime commuting distance from London.

Four miles further on, Hitchin Yard would always be worth a look, as a couple of class 31's would be more often than not be stabled there for local trip and ballast train workings.

The 25kv electrification ended on the mainline at Cambridge Branch Junction, so beyond Hitchin, an infrequent 2 car DMU shuttle would run to Huntingdon and return crewed by drivers from the small Hitchin depot. Far removed from the superb electric, and far reaching services now enjoyed by the market towns of Biggleswade, Sandy and St Neots. My old friend and former Hitchin driver John Williams had many of his early driving turns on such workings and well remembers the envy he felt looking out of his DMU window at London, Leeds, Doncaster and Gateshead drivers flying past in their Deltics on the roaring main with hardly a sideways glance at such lesser mortals.

This next section was the first really high speed part of the trip. 100 to 105 mph running was common and speeds up to 115 could be attained if late running required it. The scenic run alongside the river Ouse and round the reverse curves at Offord Cluny was another part of the journey I never grew tired of. Even more so, when some bellowing at the expensive boats and yachts would take place along with the fat cat occupants aboard.

Huntingdon the birthplace in 1599 of Oliver Cromwell would more often than not be a calling point for the semi fasts services to perhaps collect those who had alighted from the last DMU shuttle. After passing under the A14 over bridge, the Deltic would be opened up for the climb of Stukeley bank to the mini-summit at around Abbotts Ripton with the well known cold war airbase at Alconbury close by.

Connington, with its civil engineers tip, along with Stilton Fen and the village of cheese fame to the west would all add to the changing landscape as the flatter Fens gave way to the outskirts of Peterborough. Our train would begin to slow for the 40mph turnouts into the platforms, Fletton Junction would trail in from the left and at certain times of day a 47 or 56 could be seen awaiting passage onto the mainline with a train of fly ash wagons destined for the Midlands.

After arriving in Peterborough station, class 31's may been seen on the Norwich to Birmingham workings or if you were lucky and depending on the time of day then the class 37 hauled Harwich to Manchester boat train would add to the variety of observable English Electric traction. After getting back on the move, heads would be turned towards the stabling point (which very rarely may have contained a wandering or failed 55) before the vast complex of New England yard and its huge eclectic variety of engineer's wagons. Peterborough was also the home station of one of the senior bashers Tony Wardle. He would always greet you with a big smile and a bellow as he stood briefcase in hand waiting for the train to draw to a halt.

With the Deltic now working hard on the climb to Stoke Summit it would be back to admiring the wonderful scenery in this part of the country. Whilst at the same time looking out for anything of interest on the slow lines or even perhaps one of the dwindling numbers of Class 44 'Peak' locomotives on the daily Toton to Whitemoor goods train. Further up the bank the Mallard Pub at Little Bytham was always worth a bellow at as was the small plaque at the location of Mallards record breaking 126mph set in 1938. The four track section would reduce to two for the passage on the 880 yard long Stoke Tunnel (also ideal for dark hours logging as 18 seconds through the tunnel would signify 100mph on the clock.

After cruising down the bank, next came the market town of Grantham with its wonderful old world station and of course the home town of Margret Hilda Thatcher. The sidings just south of the station on the downside would host the occasional Deltic when the daily Grantham commuter train would be lucky enough to be hauled by the King of the Diesels. In the evenings or at weekends, local legends Steve Philpot or Pete Toulson could often be seen waiting to join the train and more bellowing would be in order if **ALYCIDON** or **TULYAR** was the hauling locomotive.

After roaring through Peascliffe tunnel, the Deltic would pick up speed down grade to the flat lands of the Trent valley. This was another section where very high speeds could be achieved if needed or on the odd occasion just for the hell of it. We would always look out for senior Deltic man Gordon Lacy on duty at Newark Northgate station or the most senior basher of all the 'Captain' Peter Manning on the platform waiting to join us.

The journey onwards to Doncaster was in my opinion one of the less inspiring stretches of the trip, however, by now my mind would be wandering as to what move to make at Doncaster or York and therefore more time would be spent on reflection than window gazing. High Marnham and West Burton power stations along with Bevercotes colliery would be close to the line on the downside as would Sherwood Forest and the former Chesterfield to Lincoln line which once crossed the mainline at Dukeries Junction. The name deriving from the amount of ducal estates the area once contained.

After passing the village of Rossington and its colliery the train would begin its approach to Doncaster after passing the Potteric Carr wetlands, the large Decoy and Belmont yards and of course Doncaster TMD (former 36A) which could also house any Deltics going to/from works. Finally after passing under Hexthorpe Bridge it would be a case of collecting your belongings, looking out for any Deltics in the works reception sidings before alighting in Doncaster with the 156 milepost from London midway down platform 4. No two trips would ever be the same of that I am certain.

However, back to the bash, it had been a real fortnight of highs and lows with some moves which would by the following year not even have been considered. I had learned some hard lessons one of which was not to go blind into a move that had no obvious escape route and also it was often better to stick with a Deltic hauled train than to go looking for other machines which may not have even been in service that day. That said I had some experiences to take home, the weather had been superb and my appetite wetted for further adventures. The usual 86/47 move home on the *Royal Highlander,* with the sauna bath temperatures from the ETH sending me into a deep and sweaty sleep.

55009 ALYCIDON takes a breather and boiler water at Newcastle Central with an up overnight service as the lights of Tyneside twinkle in the background.

Number 9 gets away from Edinburgh and passes Portobello FLT in the Summer of 1977.

D9021 awaits departure from Portobello FLT with the Euro-Scot inaugural run on 7/10/68.

Forever Autumn- 1980

My autumn holiday chasing Deltics in 1980 was only a week long instead of the more usual two. 55010 languished in works having its final classified repair so I took the opportunity of spending the first week of my holiday travelling mainly in the company of Darlington based Chris Short to other parts of the UK network. Over the course of the week we enjoyed loco haulage in East Anglia, North Wales, on London Bridge commuter trains, into Cornwall and even steam heat overnight trains deep into West Wales. It was only on Sunday after returning to Grantham from Skegness following some class 20 action did I decide it time to get back down to business of building my Deltic mileage. I didn't have to wait long as at 1540 or thereabouts 55002 arrived with the 1405 ex Kings Cross so I was right away Doncaster for 55021 on the 1650 up from Hull and another 156 miles back to London. I still have really strong memories of the southbound trip. The rear TSO was almost deserted and by sitting on the down side I enjoyed watching the ASH at the head of our train snaking round the numerous curves on its journey up to London as the glorious late summer evening sun shine lit up the flanks of the Deltic and its blue and grey stock. Kings Cross must have been desperately short of power as locomotives were being shunt released from inbound services to form the next northbound departure and such was the state of affairs that 1L22 left at 2300 for Leeds with a single steam heat 31 at its head. I finally managed to escape the mayhem with another 393 miles of 55021 this time bagged on the 2355 *Night Capitals* and a decent night in a sleeper berth after the previous few nights of little sleep in open stock. I had by this time secured privilege rate travel as an employee of the BRB so the when all else fails sleeper option was now more readily available to me. My sense of satisfaction was short lived as upon arrival in Edinburgh it was noted that Haymarket was Deltic free and therefore the 47 which had worked north on the previous night's 1S72 was probably going to stick to diagram and therefore 1V93 would Strum which sadly it did. All was not lost though as the Deltic which had worked the previous night's *Night Aberdonian* must surely have disappeared to Dundee and 1E10 through to London. At this point let me say that I was young, bold and didn't always think things through in a way that I would now. The sensible thing to have done next would have been to wait in Edinburgh for 1E10 but I was having none of it. I quickly worked out it would be possible (in theory) to take a DMU to Inverkeithing for a plus 5 onto the Dundee starter and an additional 13 miles along with a Deltic over the Forth Bridge. How wrong could I have been, without boring the reader with details all I will say is the unit failed at South Queensferry and we were still sat there as 55014 and its train ran majestically through the station without stopping of course. This definitely went down as my biggest bowl out yet and my whole day began to fall apart and my options to recover the situation diminishing rapidly. I really needed to think on my feet and it didn't take long to work out that I needed to get back to Edinburgh and quick. By the time the next local service had taken me back to Edinburgh any hope of catching 1E10 was long gone. However all was not totally lost as I knew 1E10 was booked slow line between Thirsk and York to allow following HST's to overtake it and therefore arrive into York first. So that's how I came to have my first ever Edinburgh to York HST trip before thankfully re-joining 55014 at this location. I sat quietly fuming at my earlier greed and don't really remember much of the trip to Kings Cross other than we left York 3 late and arrived in 4 London late after a fairly lack lustre performance from Deltic 14. Somewhere along the way we passed 55003/8/18 on northbound trains. Normal service was resumed with a trip to Doncaster behind 55006 to be followed by a wonderful Kings Cross man going home romp south with **BALLYMOSS**, a 3 late departure being turned into a 3 early arrival and some fine 110mph running as was often customary on this train. Another trip to Edinburgh followed in a sleeper berth on the *Night Capitals* with another former Scottish Deltic this time with 55013 **THE BLACK WATCH** in charge. I can't even begin to describe the joy of shutting yourself away in a snug steam heat berth in the leading SLEP right behind a Class 55 with many hours of immense pleasure and of course much needed doss ahead of you. If you did it you will know what I mean and if not all I can say is you've missed one of life's simple pleasures and all for less than £60. Arrival in Edinburgh was on time at 0645 as would be expected on the 6 hour 50 minute schedule calling only at Newcastle for a crew change.

The morning of September 9th saw Paul Gildersleve (who had travelled up on an earlier service) and I undertake the Dunbar fill in move (Deltic commuting 70's style), 55011 to Dunbar for 55008 back set us up nicely, for a run to York with **THE BLACK WATCH** on the Plymouth for an onwards run to London behind **CREPELLO** on the 0910 ex Dundee (a photo of which can be found in the book Deltics by Murray Brown). Another traditional south end weekday leap followed with 55016 on 1L45 to Doncaster, another fast run to London on 1A34 this time behind 55019 for the rancid Doncaster overnight with 55017 on 1L22 and 55009 on 1E35. Paul and I set off north on 1S12 with 55022 singing away sweetly up front. At Retford we must have gone our separate ways with Paul sticking with RSG and myself leaping for an up road run with **MELD** on the *Hull Executive* and an on time arrival in London at 1002 after a most enjoyable trip amongst the business types all booted and suited for a day in town. Things had been going too well and for the rest of the day the bowl outs came thick and fast. I had to fester in London for 1D02 at 1205 and despite the train producing another 'domino' Deltic with 55008 doing the honours; another trip to Hull mustn't have appealed as I bailed at Doncaster to be bowled with a hideous 47416 on 1E10. The strum box was already 15 late and managed to drop another 4 minutes to Newark where I cut my losses and got off in the hope 1L43 would produce the diagrammed Deltic. It did, however, **MELD** rolled in late with an ominous silence from one of its power units. Steve Philpot was already on board and confirmed **MELD** wouldn't be working back with 1A31 so there was no point going past Doncaster. After hanging about for the best part of an hour we boarded 1A28 ex Hull for another trip south this time to Peterborough and a leap from 55008 onto 55009 back to Doncaster, for another superb up road run right through to Kings Cross with **QUEEN'S OWN HIGHLANDER** on the last up stopper. Number 4 and its enterprising driver managed to turn a 12 minute late departure from Doncaster into a 2 minute early arrival in London. However, all the Deltic hauled overnights had left before we arrived at 2253 so once again it was to be a waiting game.

A sleeper berth was obtained for 1N00 and I was delighted to have another berth this time right behind 55004 which had been given a quick turn round from its previous working. I was in such a state, that I dossed right through the shunt at Newcastle and we were well into the Borders before I awoke. The booked 26 minutes in Edinburgh allowed time for a (quick) shower, take away breakfast before another former 64B machine on the Plymouth with 55016 doing the honours. Today was a day for playing safe, as the previous days antics were fresh in my mind and certainly not something I would wish to repeat. 55016 to York, back to Edinburgh on 1S27 before a doss to the Cross with the **BALLYMOSS** on 1E35 made for a solid and very high mileage 1198 mile day. Why couldn't every day be this good? Although as usual events would soon conspire against me and once again bring me crashing down to earth.

1S12 was one large and hideous Duff so a long and dreaded fester from 0430-0805 was eased by a couple of trips round the circle line and a sit down breakfast in the greasy spoon cafe near St Pancras had me ready for another day on the road. It was my initial intention to do a Hull and back. However as we left London the 55017 was backing down onto the

55017 is seen taking a breather at a very quiet Kings Cross after another trip from the North.

morning Cleethorpes service. My Lords! Therefore it was Stevenage only with 18 and then off to the seaside with 17 for a 90 minute fester 1145-1313 to take in the sea air. On easy 47 timings we arrived in London slightly early at 1658 so would in theory have made 1D04 but for reasons forgotten about we let number 11 go without us. Power must still have been tight as **BALLYMOSS** was turned round off 1A18 to work north again on 1L45 departing at 1805. I don't know where all the ETH 47's had gone but this was the only day I can ever remember when all Cleethorpes trains bar the first one up were Deltic hauled. 55021 worked the 1305 ex London and back and 55017 went back to Cleethorpes for a second time later in the day with 1D06. After having **BALLYMOSS** to Doncaster we had number 2 up road on 1A34 but tonight only to Peterborough as I wanted to cover the full selection of overnights. However, nothing produced, apart from 55008 on 1L22 so it was 8 to Retford for 16 up to London on 1E35. My final day dawned and I decided to do some line siding as the weather was good and 8 locomotives remained out of traffic. So after leaping with KOYLI on 1S12 to Grantham, I walked out towards Milepost 103 on Stoke Bank and remained there until arriving back at the station for **ALYCIDON** and the 1550 ex York. During the course of the day I managed to capture several machines on film so I was fairly impressed with the impromptu decision. After arriving in London on 1A26 we went to the Malt and Hops for a few pints of Wadworth 6X (smile if you had 6X last night as the old saying goes) and a bite to eat. My final trip of the rover was a marathon overnight in a lovely and warm compartment behind 55021 **ARGYLL & SUTHERLAND HIGHLANDER** on 1S72. During the 9 hour 38 minute journey we went via the Joint Line, Knottingley, Washington and finally the Blyth and Tyne before arriving in Edinburgh at 0818 and a trip home to Inverness behind 40069.

Forever Autumn- 1981

After many happy holidays and weekends out and about with the legends it all had to come to an end, and therefore my final full week on the road began on Monday September 21st 1981. I had travelled overnight from Inverness to Edinburgh behind 47270 and found myself in a grey and overcast Waverley station just before 0700. With only a few months until the end, only 16 machines remained in traffic and locomotives such as 55018 and 55004 were running on borrowed time such was their general unreliability. Even **ROYAL SCOTS GREY** was spending as much time out of traffic as in. The BR marketing men and a certain dubious Yorkshire DJ claimed this to be the 'Age of the Train' but it certainly didn't feel like it.

The first move of the day involved 55009 **ALYCIDON** on the rancid and tatty set of coaches forming the 0718 Edinburgh to Carlisle via Newcastle. This was a new train for me in respect of its ultimate destination, although if the train was taken all the way then it would be a long wait for the return service from the Border City. With this in mind, I left Alice and her train at Newcastle and waited for the arrival of the 1050 to Edinburgh. Rail tour favourite 55002 arrived on time with 1S12 so I climbed aboard for a trip to Edinburgh and if my luck held possibly Aberdeen. Brian Grey was my travelling companion for the trip over the border and back into Scotland. Brian was at the time Newcastle based and always good for an update on which locomotives were in works or on one engine, as often after a few weeks away from the ECML things would have changed significantly.

Unusually for 1S12 we arrived in platform 11 at the Waverley to be greeted by a spoon in the loop ready to bowl us out big time by taking over for the 130 mile trip to the Aberdeen. This certainly wasn't how my first day was meant to have started and with no booked Deltic departures for almost 8 hours, poor first day value from my all line rail rover was on the cards. Brian made the sensible suggestion of making for Carlisle via the WCML to at least salvage something with a trip back to Edinburgh or in his case Newcastle with number 9 and its bone shaking collection of mark 1's. The 1225 Edinburgh to Bristol got us to Carlisle in plenty of time, and an enjoyable stroll was taken around the city centre before returning to the station ready for a dose of 55009 at 1553. An anti-clockwise trip to Edinburgh filled the next 4 hours however with less than 200 miles covered it was hardly Class 55 performance at its sparkling best. Although to be fair it showed the versatility the duel brake and duel heat locomotives still had to offer.

I arrived in Edinburgh for the 3rd time in 13 hours and was extremely pleased and relieved to see 55016 already at the business end of 1E35. With its 2025 departure only half an hour away there was no time to waste in grabbing a quick bite of food before securing a compartment for the night. The objective of any trip on the first up overnight was to bag 393 miles of haulage and hope that 1S12 also produced to get the following day's moves up and running. At some point during the night (From one of the lads in Newcastle TOPS office quite possibly), I received gen that a one engine 55010 was allocated to 1N12 through to Tyneside. Under normal circumstances I would have let this go and stuck with my original move to London. However with so little time left and the mileage behind my machine creeping ever nearer the ten thousand mark desperate measures were needed. 1E35 and 1N12 passed each other between Newark and Retford, so it was a first but sadly not last 0230 leap at Retford. With its horse and cart schedule 1N12 was on time so my fester was kept to a minimum before heading out into the night with KOSB and into a dead end move to Newcastle. However at the time this was of no concern with another 130 miles in the book and therefore I was more than happy as we arrived in a murky Tyneside at 0530.The thought of going to Edinburgh on 1S08 never even entered my mind as I was very aware that I was now about to commence day two of my rover and had yet to manage a daylight trip south of Newcastle so it took all of a minute to get the first HST south in search of Deltic daytime action. My salvation was found at York in the form of **BALLYMOSS** and the 0805 service to London.

At last a right move and the beginning of a solid days 100mph bashing behind 55018 and 55016 before finally arriving on the 'Blocks' at Kings Cross off the 1550 service from York. A quick meal in the Wimpey outside St Pancras saw me back under the train shed for another encounter with **THE BLACK WATCH** on the second Edinburgh overnight departing at 2015. I already knew 55010 would once again working 1N12 after running light engine all the way from Gateshead during the course of the day. This meant subject of course to 1E35 producing that another Retford to Newcastle move was a strong possibility. Thankfully and with hindsight fortuitously 55017 was on 1E35 and therefore the 0230 leap at Retford took place (Little did I know it but this was the last time I would ever set foot on the station again) As I climbed out of the subway number 17 could be heard accelerating hard up Gamston Bank and out into the inky blackness of the night. The sound carried on the breeze was totally captivating and lasted for minute after minute, until I assume 17 had cleared the long curve towards Eaton Wood. Once again right on cue my machine appeared out of the darkness and an empty compartment was found in readiness for the 2.5 hour trip ahead. Groundhog Day was September 23rd with the same locomotive, working the same train on the same arrival platform in Newcastle, with the same post office workers with the same barrows all lined up to collect the mails. However, standing in the gloom it was very much another flap about what to do next, my mind was soon made up once **BALLYMOSS** arrived with the 0100 sleeping car train from London. If the diagram was followed, 55018 would work forwards to Edinburgh at 0705. Thankfully the move held and my last ever trip into Scotland behind **BALLYMOSS** went into the book, with an on time arrival in Edinburgh at 0930 prompt.

This left me with exactly 20 minutes for a 20p (now £5!!!) shower in the Superloo and a take away breakfast purchased to the accompaniment of 55013 humming impatiently outside. With my nerves by now in tatters, I was determined to have a more relaxing day and therefore York and back with 1V93/1S27 was an easy decision to make. The down Plymouth arrived back in Edinburgh right time at 1805, and this allowed for a proper meal and a few beers and for a couple of hours to feel a bit normal. Number 13 must have enjoyed spending the day with me as after arriving back in the station, I was more than happy to find the same Deltic at the head of 1E35 and the prospect of another 393 miles to be banked. Tiredness was over taking me now and the thought of leaping at Retford didn't even enter my head as I settled down for some solid sleep at the dreaded 0430 Kings Cross arrival.

Into Thursday, **PINZA** produced for 1S12 giving me my 200th Deltic hauled trip of the year with 33 more to follow before the end of the first Deltic era. I left **PINZA** at Doncaster before my first meeting of the week with another machine on borrowed time, in the shape of 55011 and a trip to London with 1A08. Further trips followed with 55002/18 and 55016 all on York semi fasts and an arrival in London at 2115 and the choice of the north bound overnights. **THE KINGS OWN YORKSHIRE LIGHT INFANTRY** was allocated to 1S70 the *'Night Aberdonian'* An £8 cross border sleeping car berth saw me right away Dundee, as this was the train's first booked call, other than Doncaster and Newcastle for change of drivers and Edinburgh Waverley for an engine and crew change. I can't remember how I got back to Edinburgh (DMU probably) but it was in time for another 55013 hauled 1V93. However, on this occasion it was one way only as another dose of **PINZA** power took me south to the capital city and a chance meeting with 55004 on the 1935 to Hull. I can still remember the Friday evening train was full and standing to Peterborough and 4 made heavy weather of keeping time, and sounded as if all the years since its last classified repair were finally catching up with the old girl. Phil Wormald, Paul Monument and I all alighted at Doncaster safe in the knowledge that 55021 was following on behind with 1S60 the 2000 Kings Cross to Aberdeen. The plan was right away Edinburgh with 21. However our plans went 'tits up' when the ASH was removed from the train at Newcastle as the forwards Haymarket driver deemed insufficient fuel was available to run the next 125 miles. After being detached from the train, 55021 scuttled off to Gateshead and a 16 wheeled thing headed out of Newcastle with the now late running Aberdeen service. With no other Deltics around things looked grim as train after train was let go in the vain hope that the next one may have had a Deltic on the front.

We played this fruitless game of Deltic roulette for over 3 hours and with time running out, we decided to get on the next south bound train regardless of the power. The 0202 service to Kings Cross was reported as running 90 minutes late and as we stood on the freezing platform we heard the station supervisor shouting over to the shunter that 55021 was on its way over from the shed and would be replacing rancid 47 whatever for the trip to London.

My Lords! Another 268 miles of the ASH and the get out of jail card used to full effect. I recall 55021 being driven absolutely flat out to make up lost time and sleep was almost impossible such was the racket coming from the front end.

We hammered through the London suburbs and finally arrived in London with 45 of the lost 90 minutes regained. After a quick breakfast, a Leeds Tram was taken to Peterborough for my last ever day time run with 55011(another machine on borrowed time) on the first up York service. The week was nearly over so the rest of the day was spent building mileage, with York trips behind 55016 and 55019 before a marathon 460 mile overnight back to Edinburgh via Cambridge, Gascoigne Wood and Beattock hauled by good old 55016 **GORDON HIGHLANDER** on 1S72. And that as they say was jolly well that other than a pair of 26's home to Inverness and a return to work early on Monday morning.

The End

My last trip behind my own favourite Deltic took place on November 7th when 55010 returned me home to Scotland after a weekends bashing, and in the process took my KOSB mileage to over the ten thousand mark. Little did I know it as we arrived in the Waverley but it was to be the last time I saw number 10 with fire in her belly. Through personal choice I decided not to come out again until

December 30th by which time the ECML had taken on a macabre funeral like feeling and all of the fun of the previous years had gone. So other than a walk round to Hexthorpe Bridge to pay my final respects to my machine and one engine runs behind **ROYAL HIGHLAND FUSILIER** on the very last service train, and **ARGYLL & SUTHERLAND HIGHLANDER** being flogged to death on a very late running York service. It was all very sad and nothing like the times that had gone before most of the pleasure had gone and I was marking time ahead of the final curtain call with 55015 and 55022 a few days later.

January 2nd 1982 really was the end of an era and I had no appetite whatsoever to visit the killing fields at Doncaster Works. It would be over 4 years before I travelled on the ECML again and 9 years before I travelled though Kings Cross. Therefore, other than a 1982 visit to ride behind 55009 and 55019 in captivity on the Moors line Deltics took a back seat as a built a life and career for myself. I sorted out all of my notebooks and photographs and archived them at my parents' house where they lay untouched for over a decade. Thankfully by the time I got round to opening the box most but sadly not all had remained intact as a record of a truly memorable few years.

Other than keeping in touch with one or two of my former colleagues, being a shareholder in the resurrection of **ROYAL SCOTS GREY** and reading the bi monthly Deltic Deadline I all but abandoned my love affair with the class and

'Death' Its ECML racing days over 55001 SST PADDY awaits the gas axe. It will soon be the second member of the class after NIMBUS to be broken up for scrap.

What involvement I had was certainly passive. I did however drag my then girlfriend Yvonne Ross out to be introduced to RSG at the Inverness open day in 1986. Although from memory she wasn't impressed and we were back in the pub less than an hour later. To be fair to her it was a boiling hot day, the banter was good and the lager seemed extra cold.

Events took a new twist following a return visit to the NYMR on April 8th 1989. So much had changed in the intervening years and I recall being in awe at the vision of **ALYCIDON** in all over blue with black glass head codes. It was Leeds in 1977, Darlington and Edinburgh in 1978. So many memories came flooding back. I was hooked and my love affair with the legends was once again rekindled.

For the next few years I was a regular face on the preserved railway scene. 55016/55022 at the Severn Valley Railway, 55019 at the Mid Hants Railway and 55015 on the Midland Railway all spring to mind with only the elusive 55002 absent from my now 'Filofax' based preservation haulage book.

The passing of each and every autumn had brought the curtain down on another part of the Deltic story. Withdrawals, final runs, the end of the *Hull Executive*, the influx of HST's to nearly all of the Hull trains, the excitement of seeing a gleaming ex-works locomotives on test or awaiting to be collected from works was a thing of the past, an increase in failures and one engine running and finally schedules eased to prepare for lesser power in 1982, all contributed to much of the polish being taken away from my hobby. I for one was glad to have been part of it but not sorry to mark its passing.

York driver Harry 'odd socks' Wilson poses with number 19 upon arrival at York with the very last service train of all.

55008 CREPELLO leaves Huntingdon with a north bound semi fast in late summer 1979. It was the last FP machine in traffic without white cabs at this time.

An unidentified Deltic departs Newcastle for London in February 1978.

At the other end of the working cycle. 55009 ALYCIDON awaits its fate

Chapter 2

My Machine

We all had our favourite Deltic and more often than not the reasons for choosing were purely personal and possibly not able to stand up to rational scrutiny. Living in Scotland it was always on the cards that my favourite Deltic would be a Scottish Regiment. In the early days I took to **ROYAL SCOTS GREY** as it was more often than not the Deltic I would always bump into when out and about. My first sighting of the locomotive which would go on to become my machine was on July 12th 1977. A days spotting in Darlington began with the arrival of 1S12 just before 1100 and I must say Number 10 looked every bit the part as it arrived under the train shed roof complete with *Silver Jubilee* headboard. During the Christmas holidays in 1978, I managed to get up close with 55010 on a more regular basis and so began an obsession that's never really ended. In January 1979 John Scott and I spent a day photographing Deltics in Edinburgh, we happened to be in Princes Street Gardens when number 10 passed by on its way to Haymarket for servicing after working the 0900 ex London. Later the same day we witnessed its departure back South with the 1700 hours and my allegiance to this superb locomotive was complete. From then on whenever I was about number 10 seemed not to be and it wasn't really until late summer did I begin to build up significant mileages and from then onwards my mileage just went up and up. However, by the start of 1980 the locomotive was beginning to look uncared for as its last classified Intermediate had been in 1976 and an uncertain future beckoned.

In hindsight 55010 was an ideal choice as my machine. My retirement home is firmly within the former recruiting area for the regiment and in fact the town of Hawick had its own territorial battalion many years ago. The KOSB's went on to serve in numerous campaigns from the defence of Edinburgh during the Jacobite rising, right up until the first Gulf war and conflicts in Iraq prior to the Regiment's amalgamation with the Royal Scots in 2006. The Regimental museum is still located in the town of Berwick upon Tweed although the last time I paid a visit they no longer had the nameplate from the Deltic and the gentleman I spoke to claimed it had been sold on some years previously. Although whilst researching material for this book I have been told by an enthusiast that they do still have the nameplate in the museum but it is no longer on public display.

What follows is a pictorial tribute to a very fine locomotive along with a tabulated summary of all my trips behind 55010. Perhaps some readers of this book may have been on the same train as my machine and I.

55010 awaits departure from Berwick upon Tweed with the Berwick to Plymouth service on July 4th 1979. This train started at Berwick during the Penmanshiel diversions.

55010 and a class 47 approach Doncaster from the North in June 1978. My machine was on the 1020 service ex Newcastle and the 47 possibly on a Leeds job.

An ex works KOSB awaits a return to traffic after its final classified repair in 1980 (Late Bob Peach).

55010 at Darlington with the Saturday 1E35 8/3/80.

Number 10 rolls into Hull with 1D04 on 2/7/79

Year 1979	Train	Run
June 4th	1205 Kings Cross-Hull	Kings Cross-Newark
June 8th	2015 Kings Cross-Edinburgh	Peterborough-Edinburgh via Carlisle
July 5th	2100 Newcastle-Kings Cross	Doncaster-Kings Cross
July 10th	1605 Kings Cross-York	Kings Cross-Newark
August 6th	1550 York-Kings Cross	Doncaster-Grantham
August 8th	2015 Kings Cross-Edinburgh	Doncaster-Darlington
August 10th	2230 Edinburgh-Kings Cross	Newcastle-Peterborough
September 17th	1410 York-Kings Cross	York-Huntingdon
September 18th	1705 Kings Cross-Hull	Kings Cross-Retford
September 20th	1810 York-Kings Cross	Doncaster-Kings Cross
September 21st	0550 Kings Cross-Aberdeen	Kings Cross-Retford
September 22nd	0606 York-Kings Cross	Selby-Kings Cross
September 25th	1705 Kings Cross-Hull	Kings Cross-Hull
September 25th	2100 Hull-Doncaster	Hull-Doncaster
September 26th	1605 Kings Cross-York	Huntingdon-Newark
December 1st	1405 Kings Cross-York	Peterborough-Doncaster
December 1st	1810 York-Kings Cross	Doncaster-Kings Cross

In 1979, I was still finding my feet and getting started. In the early part of the year it was more a case of how far can I go with the money I've got? Kings Cross to Newark on June 4th was with a day return from Kings Cross. After arriving in Newark, my wait was a short one as in no time at all, 55022 arrived with the lunch time train from Cleethorpes so it was all aboard and straight back to London. July 10th, was a Saturday leap with my machine on a 90mph set of vacuum braked stock, not that it seemed to slow the London based driver down one single bit. 55015 **TULYAR** took me back to London before a marathon trip to Edinburgh with 55006 diverted via Carlisle.

August 6th was a silly move, 55010 to Grantham before leaping blindly onto 1L44 the 1734 to York, which fortunately produced number 6 for the trip to York and back. August 10th was a dead end move to Darlington for a Class 46 on the 0139 to London. Thankfully the rejection of the Peak, led to a good dose of number 9 which was hot on its heels at 0155.

By 1980, I had privilege rate staff discount travel, so the moves I was making were much more substantial and more often than not, any time I was out bashing it was with a go anywhere rail rover. The March 10th trip was notable in that after coming home with 55010 overnight, I was just arriving at Haymarket TMD for work when she roared past working the 0855 Edinburgh to Aberdeen. A fair few Deltic bashers were on board but the best I could manage was a trip in from Haymarket on the return from Aberdeen later in the day. March 8th/9th were both maximum mileage overnights and to be frank, I just happened to be in the right place at the right time. I also note that I had at least one trip with my machine for the first half of the year. Not bad for someone who lived in the Highlands of Scotland.

As you may have read in my other book, 'Another Lifetime of Deltic locomotives' that I did not venture out onto the ECML much over the summer of 1980 and with number 10 in works for its final classified repair it would be the end of October before we met again. However, it was a real pleasure to catch up with a gleaming Deltic as it rolled into Newark with the Saturday evening service from Hull.

Year 1980	Train	Run
January 26th	1630 Aberdeen-York	Edinburgh-York
February 14th	1735 Newcastle-Edinburgh	Berwick-Edinburgh
February 21st	1707 Edinburgh-Newcastle	Edinburgh-Berwick
March 8th	2025 Edinburgh-Kings Cross	Edinburgh-Kings Cross via Lincoln
March 9th	2240 Kings Cross-Edinburgh	Kings Cross-Edinburgh
March 10th	1240 Aberdeen-Edinburgh	Haymarket-Waverley
March 10th	2230 Edinburgh-Kings Cross	Edinburgh-Darlington
March 12th	1707 Edinburgh-Newcastle	Edinburgh-Berwick
April 19th	0550 Kings Cross-Aberdeen	Kings Cross-Retford
May 31st	1734 Cleethorpes-Kings Cross	Newark-Kings Cross
June 28th	1605 Kings Cross-York	Huntingdon-York
June 28th	1956 York-Kings Cross	York-Kings Cross
June 29th	0840 Kings Cross-Newcastle	Kings Cross-Stockton via Herford Loop
October 25th	1630 Hull-Kings Cross	Newark-Kings Cross
October 26th	1005 Kings Cross-York	Kings Cross-York
October 26th	1550 York-Kings Cross	York-Grantham

Year 1981	Train	Run
January 19th	0935 Hull-Kings Cross	Doncaster-Huntingdon
January 19th	1805 Kings Cross-York	Peterborough-York
March 15th	1205 Kings Cross-Hull	Newark-Hull
March 15th	1652 Hull- Kings Cross	Hull-Kings Cross
March 17th	2025 Edinburgh-Kings Cross	Edinburgh-Kings Cross
March 18th	2300 Kings Cross-Bradford	Kings Cross-Retford
March 19th	2015 Kings Cross-Edinburgh	York-Edinburgh
June 28th	1405 Kings Cross- York	Grantham-York
June 30th	1805 Kings Cross-York	Kings Cross-Doncaster
July 2nd	1805 Kings Cross-York	Kings Cross-Doncaster
July 3rd	0910 Dundee- Kings Cross	Edinburgh-Kings Cross
July 4th	2215 Kings Cross-Aberdeen	Kings Cross-Edinburgh via Stockton/Carlisle
July 5th	1125 Edinburgh-Plymouth	Edinburgh-York via Stockton
July 7th	0940 Kings Cross-Edinburgh	Doncaster-Edinburgh
July 7th	2025 Edinburgh-Kings Cross	Edinburgh-Kings Cross
July 8th	1005 Kings Cross-York	Kings Cross-York
July 8th	1550 York- Kings Cross	York-Kings Cross
July 10th	0910 Dundee- Kings Cross	York-Kings Cross
September 22nd	0005 Kings Cross-Newcastle	Retford-Newcastle
September 23rd	0005 Kings Cross-Newcastle	Retford-Newcastle
October 3rd	1910 Aberdeen- Kings Cross	Edinburgh-Kings Cross via Leamside/Church Fenton/Knottingley/Askern/Hertford N
October 4th	1405 Kings Cross-York	Kings Cross-York
November 7th	2240 Kings Cross-Edinburgh	Peterborough-Edinburgh via Lincoln/HPJ/Normanton/Leeds/Church Fenton/Leamside/Blyth & Tyne

1981 along with that last glorious summer really pushed my mileage with 55010 to a high level. The first run of the year, from Doncaster to Hull was from memory in the company of Mr Hillingdon. 1A13 to Huntingdon for cheese and toast in the station buffet was one of his signature moves. The break from 1215 until 1253 gave us ample time to dine, have a game of two of space invaders before we headed north again this time in the company of **BALLYMOSS** to Newark on 1D02. We knew 55012 **CREPELLO** would be heading south with the mid day departure from Hull so the fester was stress free. I must add number 12 was in fine form at the time, the previous night it had whisked us south at 106mph on 1E35 and on the earlier trip north with 1D00, it had once again gone into overdrive with some very high speeds.

Our optimism for bailing at Newark was sound and in no time at all, **CREPELLO** was taking us back south at 114mph on 1A18 with the grace that only a racehorse could muster.

In March, I did a 7 day all line rover and managed to scoop some great runs with a high performing number 10. I was extremely jammy on the 19th as 55008 was removed from 1S66 at York and for a few anxious moments I thought I may need to bail if the wrong replacement traction were to back down. In fact the replacement traction was just perfect and my machine whisked us to Edinburgh with its steam heating boiler working to perfection.

In June/July, I had my last ever 2 week bash and just about everywhere I went 55010 seemed to be there. I remember someone joking that the loco was so prevalent that perhaps it had been cloned. The real highlight was on July 4th, Independence Day. Number 10 took a number of us north to Edinburgh on the sleeping cars only *Night Aberdonian* with the added bonus of a trip over Beattock for some extra mileage. The next morning I was ecstatic to find that Haymarket had chucked the loco back out for the Sunday 1V93 Plymouth train with a diversion via Stockton for some added spice. Talking of spice, a number of us celebrated with lunch in the dining car as we left Newcastle. What a civilised way to spend your time.

With time running out fast, lady luck once again shined as I fell onto 55010 on a Saturday night service out of Edinburgh with a good number of diversions due to engineering works to boost the mileage even further. The next morning in London really brought home that the end was nigh. The only Deltic to leave the capital in daylight hours was my machine on the 1405 to York. Upon arrival in York, the loco went to the depot and was not seen again for the rest of the weekend.

My final sighting of 55010 was of it dumped outside Doncaster Works as we passed by on the very last service on January 2nd 1982. I am so glad that I did not witness first hand its destruction at the hands of the gas axe lads. I hope you enjoyed my happy memories of an exceptional locomotive from a very long time ago. So engrained are these memories that it has felt like I was writing about events from much more recent times.

With Its working life over, 55010 is dumped on the works reception roads to await its fate

Chapter 3

Deltic Performance

Whenever I reflect about Deltic performance my mind goes back to an article written by the eminent and well respected timer of Deltic hauled trains who wrote under the pen name of his favourite Deltic **NIMBUS**, in Deltic Deadline number 08 entitled "The singer and not the song". The message I assume the writer was trying to convey in this well penned story was that often it wasn't the brilliance of the Deltic that made for a record breaking run but also the determination of the driver to make the very best use of the power at his disposal, He went on to give examples of late running trains being driven cautiously with no attempt to make up time or on time trains being driven furiously resulted in some very early arrivals. My second book *Another Lifetime of Deltic locomotives* gives a good insight into the work the class was capable of under British Railways ownership. This chapter focuses on the second mainline career and the logs are provided by my old friend Paul Gildersleve for which I am eternally grateful. The logs provided a cross section of work performed during the second mainline career and compliments nicely the logs previously published.

It must be empathised that what you are about to read can only be described as truly exceptional especially as the class was considered life expired by BR in 1981. The new owners at the Deltic Preservation Society and the D9000 fund really have shown that statement to be a hollow one. Cheers lads and lasses!!

So let's enjoy some top notch Deltic performance from the second mainline age.

55005 Mr Hillingdon's machine working the Sunday 1V93 on 1/6/80

TABLE 1

D9000 *'Royal Scots Grey'*

1Z49 08:03 King's Cross to Liverpool Lime Street

18th October 1997

12 coaches / 440 tons

m. ch.	Location	Sch.	Actual	Speed
0.00	KING'S CROSS	0.00	0.00	
1.26	*Holloway*		4.18	37
2.41	Finsbury Park	5.00	5.46	55
4.07	Hornsey		7.15	69
5.00	Alexandra Palace	8.00	8.00	74
6.37	New Southgate		9.13	73
8.28	Oakleigh Park		10.46	74
9.14	New Barnet		11.25	76
10.44	Hadley Wood		12.31	76
12.59	Potters Bar	14.00	14.14	77
14.39	Brookmans Park		15.29	87
17.56	Hatfield		17.33	100/102
20.26	Welwyn Garden City	21.00	19.08	98
			Sigs.	
23.40	*Woolmer Green*	26.00	21.35	73
25.00	Knebworth		22.45	83
26.60	*Langley Junction*		23.57	91
27.48	Stevenage	32.00	24.31	92
28.50	*Stevenage (Old)*		25.11	91
31.76	Hitchin	37.00	27.04	110/108/111
35.52	*Three Counties*		29.08	106
37.05	*Arlesey*		29.57	102
41.15	Biggleswade		32.22	101

44.10	Sandy	46.00	34.09	94
47.38	Tempsford		36.16	96/98
51.56	St. Neots		38.54	97
55.72	Offord		41.27	101
58.67	Huntingdon	57.00	43.17	90
62.00	Milepost 62		45.41	77
63.40	Abbots Ripton		46.46	86/102
67.28	Connington South		49.06	100
69.36	Holme		50.24	93
72.66	Yaxley		52.38	80
				SL
75.10	Fletton Junction	69.00	55.41	25
		Signal	58.02	
		Stop	67.00	23
76.27	PETERBOROUGH	81.00	69.14	
0.00	PETERBOROUGH	0.00	0.00	FL
1.53	New England North		4.14	48
3.22	Werrington Junction		5.40	70
5.43	Helpston		7.31	80
8.38	Tallington	9.00	9.37	89/91

TABLE 1 (continued)

D9000 'Royal Scots Grey'

1Z49 08:03 King's Cross to Liverpool Lime Street

18th October 1997

12 coaches / 440 tons

m. ch.	Location	Sch.	Actual	Speed
12.26	Essendine		12.11	90
15.70	Little Bytham		14.30	92/87
20.65	Corby Glen		17.49	89
23.64	Stoke Summit	21.00	19.54	86
24.77	High Dyke		20.42	94
25.63	Great Ponton		21.13	97/107
29.08	Grantham	25.00	23.10	103/100
33.27	Barkston South Junction	28.00	25.41	103/102
35.20	Hougham		26.48	103/97
39.03	Claypole		29.06	99
43.65	Newark North Gate	35.00	31.55	102/100
46.51	Bathley Lane		33.35	103/104
49.78	Carlton		35.31	101
51.09	Crow Park		36.12	100
55.48	Tuxford		39.03	90
59.13	Gamston		41.22	99
61.10	Grove Road		42.54	50
				SL
62.22	Retford	48.00	44.45	30
		Signal	47.04	
		Stop	50.22	FL
65.29	Barnby Moor & Sutton		55.55	57
71.25	Bawtry		60.28	89/87
75.02	Rossington		62.50	100

76.71	*Black Carr Junction*		63.56	
79.49	DONCASTER	74.00	68.34	

Eleven months after returning to the main line and D9000 was the motive power for a Deltic Preservation Society tour from King's Cross to Liverpool Lime Street. Since the 2nd January 1982 any opportunity for a King's Cross departure is a must for any Deltic admirer as there is that something special about a run along the ECML starting at the Cross. D9000 had over 440 tons in tow so it wasn't going to be a repeat of the final years when about 270 tons was the normal load. As a consequence and not unexpected, speeds were about 10mph below the final years as far as Brookmans Park. However, with 100mph recorded at Hatfield the old times seemed as though they were back. We then suffered a signal check through the Welwyn tunnels which was typical of yesteryear when the xx:05 Deltic departure would often catch the xx:48 Class 312 EMU to Royston. Once back on the four track section D9000 got back to work and once over the top at the site of the old Stevenage station we had 20 or so miles of predominately minor downhill running ahead. The fact that D9000 bowled through Hitchin at 110mph took us all by surprise as that old feeling drifted back. We were now experiencing something that we thought was something left in our youth as D9000 whisked us along at speeds up to a maximum of 111mph! I'm sure it was an example of seeing what the old girl could do as D9000 maintained three figure speeds for about ten miles before things returned to normal. In fact the 1 in 200 climb beyond Huntingdon to milepost 62 was taken rather lethargically unless double yellows were sighted ahead. A slow line approach and a nine minute stand outside Peterborough meant that our time from King's Cross was nothing to capture the imagination but we had still made up 12 minutes on the schedule.

The climb to Stoke Summit that now followed was completed very competently for such a load and as we approached Grantham at 107mph the good times were back again! Three figure speeds were as good as maintained along the Trent Valley until the climb started just after Crow Park. However, speed never fell below 90mph and on the descent we just missed out on another three figure speed before going through the platform road at Retford and coming to a stand to allow the modern day trains to pass. Whilst stopped just north of Retford the opportunity was taken to watch a local football match that was in progress. We were stopped for just over three minutes before our journey north resumed and on the downhill section past Rossington we again attained 100mph. An arrival in Doncaster saw us make up another five and a half minutes on schedule, bringing to the end our high speed running for the outward journey.

TABLE 2

D9009 *'Alycidon'*

1Z45 08:03 King's Cross to York

Saturday 22nd May 1999

9 coaches / 331 tons tare

m. ch.	Location	Sch.	Actual	Speed
0.00	KING'S CROSS	0.00	0.00	
1.26	*Holloway*	5.00	3.11	46
2.41	Finsbury Park	6.00	4.25	64
4.07	Hornsey		5.50	74
5.00	Alexandra Palace	8.00	6.33	81

6.37	New Southgate		7.39	79
8.28	Oakleigh Park		9.06	81
9.14	New Barnet		9.42	82/81
10.44	Hadley Wood		10.43	82
12.59	Potters Bar	13.00	12.20	83
14.39	Brookmans Park		13.30	93
17.56	Hatfield		15.28	104/106
20.26	Welwyn GC	17.00	16.59	101
23.40	*Woolmer Green*	19.00	18.53	100/99
25.00	Knebworth		19.47	101
26.60	*Langley Junction*		20.48	105
27.48	Stevenage	22.00	21.18	102
			Sigs.	71
28.50	*Stevenage (Old)*		22.06	75
31.76	Hitchin	24.00	24.27	97
35.52	*Three Counties*		26.38	110
37.05	Arlesey		27.25	108/106/112
41.15	Biggleswade		29.39	111
44.10	Sandy	35.00	31.17	108/111
47.38	*Tempsford*		33.08	108/107
51.56	St. Neots		35.29	108/109/106
55.72	*Offord*		37.49	108/106
58.67	Huntingdon	49.00	39.26	108
62.00	*Milepost 62*		41.17	100
63.40	*Abbots Ripton*		42.09	105/109
				SL
67.28	*Connington South*		45.41	40
		Signal	52.54	
		Stop	53.49	FL

m. ch.	Location	Sch.	Actual	Speed
69.26	Holme		55.43	40
72.56	Yaxley		58.57	75
75.00	Fletton Junction		60.41	86
76.27	Peterborough	64.00	61.36	90
78.00	New England North		62.41	94
79.49	Werrington Junction		63.41	97
81.70	Helpston		67.10	21
		Signal	68.20	
		Stop	68.46	
84.65	Tallington	69.00	73.27	69

Continued

D9009 'Alycidon'

1Z45 08:03 King's Cross to York

Saturday 22nd May 1999

9 coaches / 331 tons tare

m. ch.	Location	Sch.	Actual	Speed
88.53	Essendine		76.27	83
92.17	Little Bytham		78.55	87/86
97.12	Corby Glen		82.20	87
100.11	Stoke Summit	78.00	84.22	86
101.24	High Dyke		85.08	95
102.10	Great Ponton		85.39	98/108
105.35	Grantham	82.00	87.33	106/103
109.54	Barkston South Junction	84.00	89.56	108
111.47	Hougham		91.01	105/103
115.30	Claypole		93.11	107
			Sigs.	34
120.12	Newark North Gate	91.00	97.05	47

122.78	Bathley Lane		99.39	78
126.25	Carlton		102.02	92
127.36	Crow Park		102.46	94/95
131.75	Tuxford		105.44	89
135.40	Gamston		108.00	100
137.37	Grove Road		109.07	108
138.49	Retford	103.00	109.46	106/110
141.56	Barnby Moor & Sutton		111.29	107/110
143.78	Ranskill		112.45	110
147.52	Bawtry		114.51	102/100
151.29	Rossington		117.03	106
153.18	Black Carr Junction		118.07	103/99
155.76	Doncaster	117.00	119.45	101
158.02	Arksey		120.58	103/105
160.23	Shaftholme Junction	119.00	122.16	103/97
163.02	Moss		123.56	99
165.74	Balne		125.41	100
169.20	Templehirst Junction	125.00	127.40	101
172.43	Selby Canal		129.37	102/101
175.00	Hambleton North Junction	128.00	131.03	102/103
178.00	Stoker Wood		132.48	102/103
180.29	Ryther Viaduct		134.11	102/103
182.78	Colton Junction	133.00	135.42	102
184.63	Copmanthorpe		136.45	105
186.47	Chaloners Whin		137.48	95
188.40	YORK	139.00	141.31	

The return to main line running of D9009 and 55019 on 22nd May 1999 was arguably the greatest day in Deltic preservation which in my mind seems impossible to better. Both Deltics were to make a return run from King's Cross to York in the day. Just like the old days of our youth! D9009 was to work the first return trip with a 08:03 departure. The run suffered from delays and on the return run a Signal Passed at danger (SPAD) occurred causing more delay. In contrast the afternoon run with 55019 had a run with only very minor delay and consequently reached York non-stop in a shade over 124 minutes.

Quite possibly this was the fastest ever Deltic time between King's Cross and York. It justifiably received all the plaudits in the railway press in the aftermath of Deltic Super Saturday! But what did D9009 get up to? Let's take a look.

Our load was one of 9 vehicles and was only one more than the normal load experienced in the final years of Deltic operation on BR. The departure out of King's Cross, apart from being emotional for many, was highly competent with a decent exit through suburbia. Passing through Hatfield at 104mph was fantastic and with a clear run through the Welwyn tunnels it wasn't until just through Stevenage when our progress was hampered by adverse signals. However, once clear signals beckoned us on D9009 was back on full power and the descent out of Hertfordshire began. D9009 galloped through Three Counties at 110mph and with speed falling to 106mph after Arlesey, where there is a slight rise, we then attained our maximum for the day of 112mph just before Biggleswade! In fact, other than speed dropping to 100mph at the top of the 1 in 200 climb to milepost 62, D9009 was running at 106mph plus for approximately thirty miles! At Connington South we were diverted onto the slow line and stopped just before Holme to allow a Class 365 EMU and a Class 90 on the 08:10 King's Cross to Leeds to pass us. I'm quite sure that they were not catching us but we were scheduled to be overtaken so that's what happened. Once the electric traction had passed we resumed our journey north with 97mph attained at Werrington Junction before another signal stop. Word on the train was that there was a problem with one of the level crossings which are to be found in abundance along this stretch. Once on our way again we had the climb to Stoke Summit ahead and D9009 breasted the top of the gradient at 86mph. On the descent towards Grantham D9009 attained 108mph before passing Grantham at 106mph. Speed was kept between 103-108mph until a signal check approaching Newark saw speed drop to 34mph. Beyond Newark the line is fairly level and a maximum of 95mph was attained before a minimum of 89mph on the 1 in 200 climb past Tuxford. Once we were dropping down the 1 in 200 past Gamston we were back to 100mph and D9009 kept on giving. We stormed through Retford at 106mph with the Class 90 and it's Leeds train in the platform and out of our way! Our Racehorse continued the gallop with 110mph being attained on more than one occasion with speed remaining in three figures as we climbed past Bawtry. We reached 106mph on the descent past Rossington and Doncaster was treated to the spectacle of a Racehorse passing through on the centre road at 101mph! Definitely one of those occasions, when you wanted to be in more than one place at the same time. Speed remained above 100mph virtually all the way to York and our arrival in a time some 17 minutes longer than what 55019 would achieve later tells you why that run received the acclaim. However, only now when enough water has passed under the bridge can we fully appreciate what D9009 **ALYCIDON** achieved on that great day.

TABLE 3

D9009 'Alycidon'

1Z65 15:26 Stirling to Crewe

Saturday 17th July 1999

10 coaches + 55019 (DIT) / 462 tons tare

m. ch.	Location	Sch.	Actual	Speed
0.00	NEWCASTLE	0.00	0.00	
0.41	King Edward Bridge North Junction		2.38	28

2.45	Low Fell		5.05	68
5.35	Birtley	7.00	7.16	77
8.22	Chester-le-Street		9.24	82
10.11	Plawsworth		10.48	78/83
14.02	Durham	15.00	13.41	75*
21.19	Tursdale		18.49	89
23.16	Ferryhill	23.00	20.06	93
25.73	Bradbury		21.50	96/102
30.49	Aycliffe		24.40	85*/96
36.08	Darlington	32.00	28.10	94
38.57	Croft Spa		29.49	98/97
41.20	Eryholme		31.22	98
46.35	Danby Wiske		34.29	103
50.20	Northallerton	42.00	36.42	102/105
53.52	Otterington		38.41	103
58.01	Thirsk	48.00	41.10	105/106/104
62.18	Sessay		43.33	105/106
64.16	Pilmoor		44.40	103
66.66	Raskelf		46.15	100
68.78	Alne		47.29	105
70.48	Tollerton	57.00	48.25	105/106
74.56	Beningborough		50.44	105
78.46	Skelton Junction		53.03	86
80.16	YORK	68.00	56.14	

The second DPS tour again saw both D9009 and 55019 in use although I believe this was the last time it was done. This was the Crewe to Stirling tour which saw D9009 work the train from Crewe to Newcastle with 55019 dead in tow. At Newcastle D9009 came off and retired to Heaton allowing 55019 to continue alone. The same procedure occurred on the way home and it is to the final leg of the journey that we now look. D9009 took its place at the head of the train with 55019 tucked inside with both engines shut down for the return. The load for the day was 10 vehicles with a tare weight of 362 tons plus the additional 100 tons of 55019 giving a load of 462 tons tare. The Edinburgh to Plymouth train that the Deltics worked between 1979 and 1981 would often load to 13 vehicles at about 435 tons tare, so this load for D9009 was almost the equivalent of load 14.

We had the expected slow start across the King Edward Bridge before dropping down past Low Fell where D9009 accelerated this massive train up to a maximum speed of 82mph on the slight level at Chester-le-Street. Speed then dropped to 78mph on the 1 in 150 climb past Plawsworth before a respite allowed us to reach 83mph before the Durham restriction was observed impeccably. An excellent climb away from Durham saw speed held before the following downgrade at 1 in 150 allowed us to reach 89mph as we reached the start of the short climb at Tursdale. Passing Ferryhill D9009 showed that the Racehorse was in fine form with 93mph attained before the 1 in 203 drop past Bradbury and beyond allowed us to reach 102mph. The curves at Aycliffe were shown respect before D9009 was unleashed towards Darlington.

The 90 restriction past Darlington was shown a suggestion of respect before D9009 set about the famous racing stretch with its monster train in tow. We had passed Darlington in the fantastic time of 28 minutes 10 seconds having gained almost four minutes on schedule. With the Plain of York ahead D9009 produced a wonderful performance and by Danby Wiske, just over 10 miles south of Darlington, speed had reached 103mph. From this point on we were treated to Deltic running of the highest order with speed kept between 100 and 106 for the following 30 miles! When D9009 brought its train to a stand in York in a time of 56 minutes 14 seconds from Newcastle there was no doubt that we had experienced one of the great Deltic runs. It's fair to say that no other diesel locomotive could have equalled the performance that evening of the 38 year old D9009 **ALYCIDON**. Nearly 18 years after being withdrawn from British Rail Deltics were still top dogs, of that there can be no doubt.

TABLE 4

55019 'Royal Highland Fusilier'

1Z65 06:20 Crewe to Stirling

Saturday 17th July 1999

10 coaches / 362 tons tare

m. ch.	Location	Sch.	Actual	Speed
0.00	NEWCASTLE	0.00	0.00	
0.47	Manors		2.02	33
1.57	Heaton		3.27	54
4.72	Forest Hall		6.27	75
7.61	Annitsford		8.32	87
9.72	Cramlington		9.57	93
11.44	Plessey		10.59	97/99
13.74	Stannington		12.26	98
16.50	Morpeth	19.00	14.48	49*
18.44	Pegswood		16.47	75
20.17	Longhirst		18.01	90
23.20	Widdrington		19.59	95
25.49	Chevington		21.27	98/100

28.41	Acklington		23.12	98/99/80*
31.74	Warkworth		25.34	87/95
34.66	Alnmouth	34.00	27.32	84*/81
37.40	Longhoughton		29.29	83/82
39.34	Little Mill		30.52	84
43.00	Christon Bank		33.12	100/97
46.00	Chathill		35.01	99/98
49.17	Lucker		36.58	100/98
51.51	Belford	48.00	38.26	99/100
54.79	Smeafield		40.29	98/101
58.52	Beal		42.40	100/98
60.67	Goswick		44.00	99/93
63.46	Scremerston		45.45	94
65.77	Tweedmouth		47.29	72*/64*
66.78	Berwick-upon-Tweed	64.00	48.23	68*
69.67	Lamberton Toll (The Border)		50.54	72/78
72.49	Burnmouth		53.09	77
74.16	Ayton		54.22	80
78.13	Reston	72.00	57.15	85/68*
83.19	Grantshouse	77.00	61.09	72*/64*/95
87.77	Cockburnspath		64.38	88*/83*
90.53	Innerwick		66.29	94/93
93.23	Oxwellmains		68.09	95
95.32	Dunbar	86.00	69.37	83*
97.37	Beltonford		71.05	85/84
101.08	East Linton		73.33	90/95
103.57	East Fortune		75.15	90/91
106.57	Drem	94.00	77.16	87/89/83
111.17	Longniddry		80.25	84/82

113.19	*Seton*		81.52	83
114.77	Prestonpans		83.16	59
			t.s.r.	40
118.21	*Monktonhall Junction*	104.00	87.26	61/59
121.06	*Portobello Junction*		89.55	73/75
123.53	*Abbeyhill Junction*		92.41	32
124.37	EDINBURGH WAVERLEY	110.00	95.03	

On the DPS tour to Stirling in July 1999, both D9009 and 55019 demonstrated Deltic supremacy on their old patch with stunning performances. 55019 was trusted with the Newcastle to Stirling leg of the tour and it is to Newcastle where 55019 started both engines before tackling the northern stretch of the ECML. Our steed had a load of 10 vehicles weighing in at 362 tons tare to take over the hardest section of the famous route which would take us across the border. A good start out of Newcastle saw us reach a maximum of 99mph before the first obstacle, which was the 50mph restricted curve through Morpeth, where we were just over four minutes to the good. The line speed had been raised in several sections of this route since 55019 last came this way and it was pleasing to see how 55019 would cope. Once away from Morpeth the gradient is undulating but not too noticeable either way. This allowed 55019 to record the first three figure speed when 100mph was attained just before Acklington. A couple of miles further on there is a restriction which saw us drop down to 80mph before we reached 95mph prior to the 85mph restriction at Alnmouth. We passed here over six minutes to the good and speed failed to increase on the 1 in 170 climb to Little Mill. After Little Mill the line soon drops at 1 in 150 past Christon Bank where 55019 whisked us up to 100mph again. Over the following 20 miles or so we had mainly favourable gradients waiting for us and 55019 was able to bowl along and or near the ton. A few miles before Berwick we had a 1 in 190 climb past Scremerston which saw speed begin to drop, but it helps as a nice speed arrester for the restriction across the Royal Border Bridge and through Berwick. By now we were more than 15 minutes to the good as we set about the 1 in 190 climb into Scotland. Speed had reached 72mph as we entered 55019's old home patch at the Border. The next section was all about full power being used to keep us going through the difficult area leading to Grantshouse. Our maximum speed along here was 85mph which was attained at Reston as we continued climbing at 1 in 200. Beyond Reston is Grantshouse and the Penmanshiel diversion which was big news 20 years earlier. Once around the deviation we descended the 1 in 96 past Cocburnspath and reached a maximum of 95mph at Oxwellmains. We passed Dunbar at just under the limit but over 16 minutes early. Over the undulating stretch beyond Dunbar speed was kept in the 90's with just a hint that we were taking things easier. A temporary speed restriction awaited us beyond Prestonpans and an easy run in to Edinburgh saw us come to a stand in a time of 95 minutes 3 seconds, some 15 minutes ahead of schedule. This was quite easily the fastest time I had ever recorded with a Deltic over this difficult road and just gives a taste of what might be possible over the full 393 mile route. With 4.5 hours Kings Cross to Edinburgh with stops at York and Newcastle well within the capabilities of the locomotives and crew. Three generations of traction later and no great strides forwards have really been attained.

		TABLE 5		
		D9000 *'Royal Scots Grey'*		
		10th July 1999		
		0658 Birmingham NS-Ramsgate		
		7 coaches / 236 tons		
m. ch.	Location	Sch.	Actual	Speed
0.00	COVENTRY	0.00	0.00	
1.19	*Humber Road Junction*		1.58	70
4.70	*Brandon*		4.30	99/101
9.58	*Flyover Junction*		7.27	76*/55*
11.39	Rugby	9.30	9.15	64
13.55	*Hillmorton*		10.59	85/91
15.17	*Kilsby North*		12.00	87
			t.s.r.	60
18.61	*Welton*		15.00	92/102
24.24	*Weedon*	22.00	18.23	100/99
26.54	*Heyford*		19.48	101/98
29.36	*Banbury Lane*		21.27	100
31.11	*Blisworth*		22.28	101
34.14	*Roade*		24.17	100/101
37.32	*Hanslope Junction*	33.30	26.13	100/101
39.20	*Castlethorpe*		27.19	100/101/99
41.47	Wolverton		28.43	100/101
44.13	Milton Keynes Central	38.00	30.15	100
47.25	Bletchley	42.30	32.08	102
49.31	*Stoke Hammond*		33.22	100/89*
53.65	Leighton Buzzard		36.12	93
55.63	*Ledburn Junction*	52.30	37.26	100/99

57.71	Cheddington		38.42	101/99
62.25	Tring	58.00	41.20	100/101
66.04	Berkhamsted		43.34	100
69.41	Hemel Hempstead		45.38	101
70.74	Apsley		46.28	100/101
73.04	King's Langley		47.44	100/99
76.44	Watford Junction	71.00	49.50	100/99
78.02	Bushey		50.43	100/102
80.55	Hatch End		52.18	101
82.49	Harrow & Wealdstone	80.00	53.27	100
85.76	Wembley Central		55.30	92
			59.09	Sigs.
			60.37	Stop
88.52	West London Junction	85.00	61.44	15*
89.38	North Pole Junction	87.00	64.28	30
			t.s.r.	32/53
91.26	KENSINGTON OLYMPIA	90.00	67.28	

When D9000 commenced working for Virgin Trains who knew where it would lead. There were many great days out for those of us who had been there before and were reliving our youth and also for those who were too young first time around it gave them a chance to enjoy a Deltic on service trains. Of course, new followers were also won over to the appeal of these mighty machines. During the summer of 1998 and 1999 D9000 had a regular Saturday job working from Birmingham New Street to Ramsgate and return. An excellent day out was on offer and from a performance perspective the morning run along the West Coast Main Line from Coventry to Kensington Olympia was enticing. The run I have chosen is from the summer of 1999 and demonstrates how the new era of Deltic drivers were just as capable of putting in a top quality performance as the footplate crews of 20 years previous.

We had the normal 7 vehicle featherweight load in tow and D9000 took full advantage of the falling gradient away from our Coventry start. In fact a speed of 101mph was attained prior to the restriction over the flyover approaching Rugby saw speed fall to 55mph. Once through the station we had a brief chance to get up some speed on the rise away from the Warwickshire town. However, just after Kilsby we had a 60mph temporary speed restriction to negotiate and once clear of the tunnel we had 30 miles ahead before the next slowing. On the initial descent towards Weedon D9000 reached 102mph but over this entire section from just after Welton to the Leighton Buzzard restriction our driver kept D9000 between 98-102mph.

This was a beautiful exhibition from our Saltley man with only gentle gradients to contend with, but with 3300hp on tap it would be easy for speed to run away with such a light load if our man took his eye off the ball. A slight touch of the brakes after Stoke Hammond in order to conform with the 90mph restriction through Linslade tunnel before power was re-applied to see us through my post-Deltic era home town at 93mph. There then followed another stretch of just under 30 miles where our driver again kept D9000 between 99-102mph. This was another top class piece of work as this section includes the slight climb to and away from Tring which could so easily have seen speed all over the place! With speed now being reduced we passed through my childhood local station of Wembley Central at 92mph with the brakes going on. A signal stop followed as we waited for a path off of the WCML and round the corner to our Kensington Olympia stop. The timings allowed for a deviation via Northampton, which did occasionally occur, but as we ran on the main all the way we came to a stand over 22 minutes early. An excellent performance from D9000 and also our Saltley driver.

With the speedometer hovering around the 100mph mark ALYCIDON flies through Peterborough with the 13:00 ex London.

And to end this chapter, a quote-It has been written before that with some of the performances the locomotives put in down the years that the gains made by purchasing HST's possibly wasn't as great as the BRB accounted for. I was once told a story of a Driver who went for his HST training. A Senior BRB Manager happened to be visiting the training venue and asked the driver if he was looking forwards to travelling at two miles per minute with the new traction. I am not sure what he made of the reply which was *"No not really as I do that with my Deltic from time to time already"*.

Chapter 4

Deltics in Scotland

So what circumstances did it take to allow this class to work off booked route? The locomotives themselves were not the issue, the low route availability of RA5 made them a go anywhere engine on most passenger lines. The major constraint was of course driver route knowledge; with only a relatively small number of men trained it did restrict the locomotives sphere of operation but not as much as the reader may think.

Possibly the best starting point when writing an article about Deltic locomotives in Scotland is an overview of how the locomotives entered the country and of course left again, more often than by the same route but not always.

The machines were built to revolutionise travel on the ECML between London-Newcastle-Edinburgh and Yorkshire. So if you didn't know that right up until withdrawal that these fine machines could be seen operating daily between Berwick-upon-Tweed and Edinburgh then it's probably best you don't read any further.

We can discount the Border Counties route between Hexham and Riccarton Junction along with the Solway Junction route between Bowness on Solway and Annan as both these lines had closed long before Deltic operation began in 1961.

The Waverley route between Carlisle and Edinburgh saw semi regular use before its untimely closure. From 1969 onwards the mainline over Beattock to became the sole surviving regular diversionary route, and saw its last Deltic on a service train pass this way in the autumn of 1981. Following a run round at Newcastle, this train hauled by **GORDON HIGHLANDER** saw yours truly in the very rear sleeper berth of the very rear coach. I can therefore boast the tenuous claim to fame of being the last person to pass over Beattock summit 55 hauled during the first mainline career.

The final Deltic to pass over the border on a service train was 55019 working the 1630 Aberdeen to York on December 31st 1981. This was the very last day of in service operations and with all locomotives (bar those needed for the farewell special) withdrawn by midnight; RHF crossed the border back into England with a little over 3 hours to go.

On March 17th 1979 during an overnight engineering possession, the roof on part of the tunnel at Penmanshiel collapsed. Works to lower the tunnel bed to accommodate container traffic was due to take place between January 21st and April 15th. Sadly the collapse took the lives of Peter Fowler and Gordon Turnbull who were working inside at the time. Following this tragic incident, the line was blocked for 5 months until a deviation was built and the line could once again become a through route. This was of course the period of the infamous and highly entertaining Dunbar shuttles. This involved regular Deltic working on short rakes of coaches running between Edinburgh and Dunbar and return with a connecting bus service to Berwick for those travelling towards Newcastle and beyond. All the serviceable machines operated the shuttles at some point, and there is a well-known event amongst enthusiasts of 55006 being worked up to 116mph on one such Saturday afternoon working, making it the fastest speed ever recorded by a Deltic in Scotland until D9000 equalled it whilst working for Virgin Cross Country in 1999. My first trip over the new line was the day after it had reopened on August 21st, and was behind **THE GREEN HOWARDS** whilst working 1S12. There is a memorial to the men who lost their lives on top of the old tunnel, worth a visit of you are ever passing by on the A1 trunk road.

I have been given some anecdotal material from a well respected and trusted Edinburgh based enthusiast that the short branch from Drem to North Berwick used to see a Deltic working a very early morning parcels/newspaper train back in the day; however, I have been unable to find anything to either prove or disprove that this indeed was the case.

What can be proven though is the visit of **ALYCIDON** to the resort to rescue a failed DMU on October 4th 1981, when number 9 took charge of the 1108 train to Edinburgh hauling the errant cart on a one way trip to Haymarket TMD.

The Edinburgh suburban lines saw regular visits on both diverted ECML services and also empty coaching stock moves (ECS) to/from Craigentinny CS. Pictures also exist of D9000 inside the former terminus station at Leith Central; the photograph which was taken in the early 1960's and was I believe a consequence of the rebuilding of Haymarket TMD from steam operation to diesel. It is a fair assumption that Deltics used both the route via Abbeyhill Junction and Piershill Junction, both of which, like the line to Leith Central closed some time ago. I have seen no evidence whatsoever which proves if Deltics ever worked over any of the other lines which once formed part of the extensive network around Edinburgh. However the thought of a Deltic working in Princes Street terminus or down to Granton or North Leith is a tantalising one.

Cardenden, was once a small mining town and more recently part of the ever growing Edinburgh commuter belt. To many new Deltic enthusiasts the name may not mean very much, however to those of us of a certain age it was one of the 'Holy Grail' destinations that we aspired to visit, but only Deltic hauled of course. The 1718 Edinburgh to Cardenden was one of the trains that would in the event of the Edinburgh area suffering from DMU shortages revert to locomotive plus 6 coaches. I have seen Deltics on the service twice, but have never managed to be in the right place to get aboard. In August 1979 we passed **ALYCIDON** as it made its way into Edinburgh with a morning Cardenden train and on February 14th 1980, **TULYAR** was observed running through the Waverley on the return empty stock from the evening service. So near but yet so far, unlike the commuter trains of today, the trains could only operate via Dunfermline as the line from Cardenden through Thornton was freight only.

Deltics did of course work further into Scotland through Fife on a fairly regular basis right up December 28th 1981 when 55008 became the final machine to work out of Aberdeen on the 1830 to Edinburgh. Prior to the introduction of HST services, workings to Aberdeen were very sporadic, such as 55019 working the 0855 Aberdeen to Kings Cross on September 6th 1974 or on March 15th 1975 when **ROYAL SCOTS GREY** worked the 1035 *Aberdonian* all the way from Aberdeen to Kings Cross a very rateable working for this era. As the years passed, it would be an unusual week that did not see at least one working to the Granite City. One of the most common diagrams was the 0550 from Kings Cross and returning with the 1630 to York. More often than not the Deltic for Aberdeen would come on at Edinburgh, usually replacing one of its class mates. However a locomotive could and did work the whole 523 miles from Kings Cross when the power situation dictated it, although fuel would be needed at Ferryhill before any further working could take place. No Deltics were ever diagrammed to work north of Edinburgh with one exception; this was of course the 0910 Dundee to Kings Cross dated service in 1980-1981. Diagram 07 saw the engine work to Dundee from Craigentinny with the empty stock running as 5E10 before taking 1E10 from Dundee all the way through to London. A trip I managed once with 55013, hellfire and very appropriate for the Dundee area.

2 Haymarket drivers have a blether following the arrival of 1S27 on 11/5/80

55017 gets away from Dundee Tay Bridge with one of the regular Deltic turns on the Aberdeen road. On this occasion the 12:40 return service from the City of Granite.

The Ladybank to Perth line via Newburgh, was a route used on the odd occasion when stock was left at Perth overnight due to engineering works or stabling capacity issues nearer Edinburgh. Several trusted and reliable sources have reported light engine Deltics including 55021 on April 19th 1978, operating this way. So I am more than happy to add this 16 mile branch to the confirmed list of workings.

Another regular route was the much lamented Cowdenbeath to Bridge of Earn line through Glenfarg, before its controversial closure in 1970, to allow the new M90 motorway to occupy the trackbed. This was the main route for Edinburgh to Perth trains and was used by the frequently type 5 hauled Anglo-Scottish car carrying train in the 1960's. This service often employed Deltic power from Holloway in North London all the way to Perth or vice versa. As an example, D9004 worked the train on May 28th 1964 from Edinburgh to Perth before being replaced by D9008 for the run south, although many other class visits are well documented. The train continued to produce from time to time until it was diverted to Kensington Olympia in 1969 and naturally operated via the WCML instead.

Prior to its closure in 1969, the original diversionary route for Deltic hauled services to Scotland was via the 98 mile route from Carlisle to Edinburgh via Hawick. Deltics would arrive in Carlisle via the Tyne Valley from Newcastle, before leaving the WCML just north of Citadel station at Port Carlisle Branch Junction. After running through the 'debatable lands', the train would climb over the Cheviots; pass through the woollen mill towns of Hawick and Galashiels the only real towns of size on the route. After some further sustained hill climbing over the Lammermuir Hills, the final long descent into Edinburgh would take place. This route saw its first Deltic on June 8th 1958 when the prototype made its first visit to Scotland and back again a few days later. Regular visits took place right up to the very last day of the lines existence on January 6th 1969. The final visit on a service train took place on Boxing Day in 1968 when the appropriately named **THE KINGS OWN SCOTTISH BORDERER** paid a visit to Hawick to work the 0658 stopping train to Edinburgh. The last Deltic to work over the whole route in daylight southbound was D9004 on 8th June 1968 on a diverted London service.

Before its closure as a through route in 1965, the line from Tweedmouth near Berwick to Kelso would also see the occasional Deltic. This offered a further variation to the theme, as if the mainline happened to be blocked between Edinburgh and Berwick upon Tweed, trains could reach Newcastle without needing to pass through the congested station at Carlisle or along the busy section from Hexham. In the lines dying days, driver route knowledge would have been a problem, and it's assumed a route conductor driver from Galashiels or Tweedmouth would be needed for any Deltic workings. Thankfully, one working has been recorded, which involved D9006 running via Kelso with a diverted Anglo-Scots train on August 8th 1961.

The most common and well documented route into Scotland for diverted Deltic hauled trains was the one via Beattock and Cobbinshaw, and thus entering Edinburgh from the west end. Trains would travel over the scenic Tyne valley route with a Gateshead driver in charge, who would then surrender his Deltic to a Haymarket man for the run to Edinburgh or in some cases pick up a Carstairs based conductor driver who would accompany the Geordie for the remainder of the trip. Trains would arrive in Carlisle station via the conventional London Road route from Newcastle, however on more than one occasion the Deltic would avoid Carlisle station all together by taking the goods line to Bog Junction, Rome Street Junction, through Dentonholme before re-joining the WCML at Caldew Junction. I know from a reliable source that 55021 took this route with a diverted sleeping car train during the Penmanshiel diversions, as did other 55 hauled trains the same night. Sadly this route was destroyed by a runaway freightliner train in 1984 and following extensive damage it never reopened.

After departure from Carlisle, The Deltic would follow the former Caledonian route over Beattock and then have a fast run down the down the Clyde Valley to Carstairs, before turning hard right thus avoiding the station. The next obstacle was the climb up to Cobbinshaw Loch, and then it was down grade to Slateford, and after passing the numerous west end breweries into Edinburgh and journeys end.However it was not always that straight forwards, and on the very odd occasion both the ECML and WCML would be blocked at the same time.

Thankfully all was not lost and a Deltic along with an adventurous crew could still get home to Edinburgh, as 55006 managed to do on December 29th 1974. Any Deltic hauled service would follow the normal diversionary route to Gretna Junction; here it would take the 50mph turn out onto the former Glasgow & South Western route through Dumfries and along the Nith Valley to Kilmarnock. After passing high above the town at 30mph the Deltic would head straight on to Lugton and Barrhead before descending into the Glasgow suburbs and down to Muirhouse South Junction and round onto the WCML at Larkfield Junction. For the next 7 miles a north bound train would be heading southwards as far as Uddingston, here the Deltic would swing east, before heading up the Bellshill Bank and making for Edinburgh via Shotts and Slateford Junction where it would join up with the route from Carstairs. Manning such a move must have been a nightmare. I suspect Carlisle drivers would be involved at least as far as Kilmarnock, with Polmadie drivers piloting the train onwards to Carfin and if the Haymarket man in charge of the Deltic was in a link that didn't include local work over the Shotts route perhaps all the way to Haymarket station itself. A trip such as this would really take a Deltic to the very limit of its fuel capability and drivers would pray for no further delays en-route used up valuable fuel reserves. A variation to the above took place in the early hours of September 29th 1979. 55011 was working north with 1S72 when for some unknown reason it was diverted through Kingmoor New Yard on the goods lines, over the flyover on the up arrival road before finally re-joining the WCML at Mossband presumably after reversing on the crossovers at this point to get back onto the down main. Pilot working, flag men and a block conversion ticket would all have been needed to keep the job running.

FIFE & FORFAR YEOMANRY passes Cobbinshaw Loch with a diverted 1E35 in the summer of 1979. Earlier the same day number 6 had been piloted by an ex-works CREPELLO on part of the run north with 1S12. The small signal box was hastily built to increase capacity during Penmanshiel closure.

The main locomotive workshop in Scotland for many years was at St Rollox in the end end of Glasgow. Most and possibly all of the Scottish based Deltics had their nameplates fitted at this location and 9010 paid a second visit when it attended the works open day in May 1973. The obvious route for locomotives to take was along the Edinburgh and Glasgow mainline, and after running over the junction at Cowlairs West the Deltic would enter the works off the down Stepps line. Locomotives could in theory have travelled via Stepps, Cumbernauld, Falkirk Grahamston and Polmont and back along the E&G from there. Sadly no verifiable evidence exists of what the actual route taken was for the visits to Springburn.

The Edinburgh to Glasgow mainline was a fairly regular host of Deltic locomotives in the 1960's with the Queen of Scots Pullman being Deltic hauled out of Glasgow Queen Street from time to time until the train's demise in 1964; one such working involved my machine D9010 on the 1100 ex Queen Street on May 26th 1962. In the final summer of the locomotives life, a number of visits to Queen Street were made including one by 55004 on July 20th.

Another unusual train which could produce a Deltic from time to time was the Edinburgh to Glasgow Salkeld Street parcels train. This eclectic mix of vans, would take a machine along the E&G, through Springburn/Bellgrove and then over the Glasgow City Union lines, before reversing through the Smithy Lye and into the former parcels depot. I believe the train was also booked to call into St Rollox works to collect or drop off DMU vehicles in need of repair. On February 17th 1980, I was in the upstairs training room at Haymarket depot receiving tuition on the safe working of trains when 55014 rumbled past the depot on its return from Salkeld Street on such a working. The large number of Deltics sitting spare in Edinburgh was no doubt a contributory factor to such an unusual working.

On September 15th 1978, the Scottish Region held and open day at Shields depot in Glasgow, 55019 was chosen (possibly because of the regiments association with the city). RHF took the above route but carried on that little bit further to Shields Junction before dropping onto the electric depot of the same name. I recall sitting in the cab at the open day, as the Corkerhill driver who was minding the loco tried to convince me a class 50 would out pull a Deltic any day. I did remind him that a pair of 50's was needed to keep time on his railway!!!

Another well documented variation on the E&G theme was the visit of 55021 to the small town of Oban. The runs took place on the 2nd and 21st of August 1981 as part of Scottish regions desire to run a Sunday tourist train from Edinburgh. The trains ran via Falkirk High, Cowlairs East, before running along the north side of the Clyde through Dumbarton and onto the West Highland Line proper at Craigendoran Junction. My second book *Another Lifetime of Deltics* covers the Oban trips in much more detail.

Look familiar? Made from one of the former Silver Jubilee headboards by Edinburgh based enthusiast John Scott.

An immaculate D9021 is seen in unfamiliar surroundings at the Eastfield Depot open day in 1972. Copyright Harry Archibald.

During the refurbishment of Craigentinny depot in 1977/78, the stock for the Edinburgh to Plymouth service was serviced overnight in Stirling. Although 1V92 (later 1V93) was not booked a 55 at this time, the Deltic for 1E05 the up *Flying Scotsman* would sometimes be dispatched to Stirling to take 5V92 to Edinburgh before taking over its booked working to London. Published photographs exist of 55019 at Stirling and of 55006 leaving Perth CS on this working.

Between Larbert and Stirling was the rail served colliery at Polmaise. This was one of the locations that the stock for the Royal Train would be stabled overnight when visiting Scotland. I have in my archives a picture of an immaculate D9021 carrying the head code 0X00 about to go onto the branch to collect the Groves stock, before taking its number 1 occupant the short distance to Stirling station. This event place on January 21st 1971 and is definitely one for the mega rare files.

In 1980 a colleague of mine who worked on the footplate at Haymarket, remembers being sent with 55018 to collect a failed 47/7 and its mark 3 stock from Falkirk. **BALLYMOSS** left the errant shove set in Springfield yard, then home of the fledgling Scottish Rail Preservation Society before taking the failed 47 back to Haymarket. Former DPS member John L Scott was there to record for posterity this unusual event although I have never seen a picture of the event in print.

Finally we turn our attention to the Highlands. Perth to Inverness saw its first Deltic power over the high mountains when D9004 visited the town for its naming ceremony in May 1964. D9019 visited to work a troop train from Inverness to Edinburgh on April 15th 1967 and finally **QUEENS OWN HIGHLANDER** paid a further visit for the depots open day on July 10th 1973. However on this occasion with a possible twist! A school friend of mines father, a man of the upmost integrity, who certainly knew his locomotives, has always claimed he saw a Deltic arriving light in Inverness off the Aberdeen line around this time. He described the nameplate as being a single line regiment, so I wonder if it was QOH that he saw on its way to the open day. If so the locomotive probably worked something into Aberdeen on the previous day following is arriving in Edinburgh on the 0800 ex KX on July 8th.

The dates and locations for the naming of the Scottish based Deltic locomotives are already well documented. However what is possibly less well known is how the locomotives got to/from the places where the naming ceremonies took place; to say some of the track was rare would be an understatement.

D9000, the locomotive was named in Edinburgh Waverley station on June 19th 1962 before working the accelerated *Flying Scotsman* to London on the first day of the full accelerated Deltic timetable.

D9004, the naming ceremony took place in Inverness on May 23rd 1964. The locomotive worked into Inverness with the *Royal Highlander* sleeping car train on the 22nd and returned light to Haymarket immediately after its naming by way of the Highland Mainline, Perth, Glenfarg and the Forth Bridge. I believe a Haymarket driver acted as traction conductor north of Perth and drove the locomotive himself to/from Perth.

D9006, the naming ceremony took place on either December 5th or 12th 1964 (both dates in public domain) at Cupar station in Fife. Number 6 is believed to have run to/from Haymarket light engine on the day of the naming.

D9010, my own favourite Deltic was the penultimate machine to be named and this was finally undertaken with Ceremony at Dumfries station on May 8th 1965.The locomotive worked light from Glasgow Works prior to the event and afterwards worked a troop train destined for Inverness with the Deltic coming off at Perth. The train left Dumfries at 1458 and ran via Kilmarnock, over the now closed route through Cunninghamhead and Montgreenan to Dalry, round the Paisley GS avoiding line, and up through central Scotland. This may go down as one of the most unique working for a Deltic in Scotland and the fact that the train carried passengers and went so deep into G&SW territory makes it in my eyes the most outrageous Scottish workings of all time. A photograph of D9010 leaving Dumfries can be found in Brian Webb's book The Deltic Locomotives of British Rail.

D9013, the superb and much missed beast had its nameplates fitted in Glasgow Works on January 15th 1963 before running light to Dundee the following day. The actual ceremony took place in the now closed Dundee West station (the science park now occupies its site). After the naming ceremony Deltic 13 returned light to Haymarket and took the long route via the coast through Anstruther and Levan. This line closed in 1965 and I suspect 13's visit was the one and only time a Deltic had passed this way.

D9016, named in Aberdeen on July 28th 1964 with locomotive working light to/from Haymarket either side of the event. **GORDON HIGHLANDER** may have been the only Scottish machine to have its nameplates fitted in England, as the locomotive paid a visit to Doncaster works between July 20th and 24th. If this wasn't the case then a visit to Springburn must have taken place between 24th and 28th.

D9019, the final member of the class to be named and this was done with ceremony at Glasgow Central station on September 11th 1965. It is assumed the Deltic had its plates fitted in Glasgow Works before running light the short distance to Central station. D9019 may also have been the only Deltic to have been named whilst running on only one power unit, after heading south light engine the locomotive entered Doncaster Works the following day for an engine change. I wonder if the politics around should it be named **ROYAL HIGHLAND FUSILIER** or **CAMERON HIGHLANDER** delayed the naming for so long and over 3 years since D9000 was named in 1962

D9021, this majestically named locomotive was named with ceremony at Stirling station on November 23rd 1963 before returning light engine to Edinburgh and an immediate return to action with a trip to London on the same days *Heart of Midlothian* service. We would have expected no less of the ASH.

My second book, *'Another lifetime of Deltics'* covers the English diversionary routes in great detail.

The Waverley Route

The Waverley Route and the Class 55's both had a life span far shorter than should have been the case. With the former closing 120 years after it opened and the latter having a life span of just over 20 years the British malaise of scrapping useful assets prematurely certainly applied in both cases.

Evidence suggests that the Waverley route was not the stranger to Deltic power that some casual observers may think. The 98 miles between Edinburgh and Carlisle was shorter and less congested than the former Caledonian Railway route via Carstairs and was for many years the main diversionary route for the ECML. 64B later Haymarket depot had a number of jobs to Carlisle including the prestigious through services to London St Pancras, still known colloquially as 'The Pullman'. So with route and traction knowledge not being a problem the stage was set for the occasional sound of 3300 horses unleashed on the 1.75 climbs over Falahill, and up the 13 mile climb to the lines summit at Whitrope. The first recorded visit other than the prototype's light engine run some years previously I can find of a loco to the route was during the extremely hard winter of 1963 when during the month of January D9000 passed Whitrope heading south with an up diverted express. The last visit was by D9007 **PINZA** on the well documented and morbid final day rail tour on January 5th 1969.

It's a grey morning at Edinburgh Waverley station in the autumn of 1967. The east end of the station is its usual busy self with much traffic passing through the platforms and shunting of carriages to form any number of departing services. Our eyes and ears are drawn towards platform 1 where an immaculate two tone green Deltic locomotive waits for the arrival of coaching stock to form the famous 10 o'clock *Flying Scotsman* service to London Kings Cross. We leave the impatient mumble of the idling Deltic behind us and walk down from our vantage point onto the concourse where we note that the passengers are beginning to board 1A23 as the excitement surrounding the departure of the 10 o'clock increases .The station tannoy is warning intending travellers that due to flooding between Grantshouse and Reston the service will today be diverted via Hawick and Carlisle adding almost 2 hours to the overall journey time. We walk towards the front of the train counting a dozen mark 1 carriages including a buffet and dining car, the whole lot weighing in at around 440 tons gross. Approaching the Deltic we note its name and number as D9009 **ALYCIDON** one of the London based machines based at 34G shed (later to become the famous Finsbury Park). Although we did not know, that in 2 months time, the locomotive would be allocated to 64B for air brake trials. However, these trials were cut short when the loco was almost destroyed by fire at Tempsford as it was heading north with an evening departure from Kings Cross.

Escaping steam is beginning to hiss through the pipe between loco and stock as the Deltics steam heating boiler begins to do its job by providing heat and hot water to the train. The right hand side door slides open and we are invited into the cab to enjoy our impromptu footplate trip as far as Carlisle. Looking round we take it the sights and sounds of our cramped surroundings, the row of lights above the driver's desk shows that both engines are running and no faults with the locomotive exist, Main air pressure is a steady 140psi and the brake gauges show we have 21" of vacuum brake pressure throughout the train. The locos straight air brake is applied with 30psi registering on each of the locomotives brake cylinders. Finally we note the Deltic is carrying circa 800 gallons of boiler water and a steady 40psi of steam is now being pumped through the train. The friendly driver introduces himself as Ted Manson, and informs us that whilst now based at 64B his career actually started as a locomotive cleaner at the small shed at Hawick way back in 1921, and therefore he has an intimate knowledge of the route we are about to travel over and will gladly share some of that knowledge with us during our time together. The signal at the end of the platform winks to green as the leather sound deadening curtain is pulled over to keep out the worst but certainly not all of the noise and draughts from entering the cab. For the next 2 hours or so we are now cocooned in our own little world.

Come the appointed hour the controller of our mighty steed is nudged open and slowly, agonising slowly we began to move away from the platform and into the north bore of Carlton Tunnel. The first 3 miles are totally uneventful and typical of any number of Deltic runs, it is only when the brakes come on and the locomotive lurched to the right over Portobello Junction and onto the Carlisle route proper that the significance of the journey began to dawn. Once clear of the mainline power is slowly applied to warm the engines thoroughly for the significant climbing ahead. After passing the recently opened Millerhill Yard a hive of shunting activity with several loco classes of EE, Sulzer and a brace of Clayton locomotives patiently waiting work, the power handle is pulled all the way open and the Napier's really start to sing and cover the south end of the yard with a dusting of milky white exhaust. Once clear of Glenesk Junction (the line to Dalkeith sadly closing the year before) we began to climb at an initial gradient of 1:200 away from the coast and into the hills. The speedometer is marching round to the lines limit of 60mph before the gradient stiffens to 1:70 at Hardengreen Junction, the line to Penicuik curving away to the right. Even for a mighty Deltic, Borthwick Bank begins to take its toll and speed balances at around 45mph for the final few miles to the first summit at 998 feet above sea level. Falahill is but a shadow of its former self with goods loops and banking sidings in the process of being lifted and only the signal box remaining standing in isolation amid the hills. With the controller now closed we can once again hold a conversation without shouting as we drop down through Heriot and Fountainhall and into the wide glacial valley of the Eldon Hills.

Skilful use of the brake is needed to keep our speed checked between 45-55 mph round the switch back valley of the Gala water. The 249 yard Bowshank Tunnel is passed just under 40 minutes after leaving Edinburgh. Speed is reduced further with the vacuum brakes checking us nicely for the approach to Galashiels and Kilknowe Junction where the line from Peebles trailed in from the right until closure in 1962. The first major centre of commerce at Galashiels and 33 miles from Edinburgh is passed in 44 minutes and 50 seconds.

Hot cups of tea freshly brewed on the Deltics hotplate is passed round as we glide through the station at a stately 30mph, catching the attention of folk waiting for the next Edinburgh bound train in only the way a Deltic can. As we pass Netherdale the home of the famous Gala RFC and cross over the river Tweed towards Tweedbank **ALYCIDON** is given her head and the mesmerising sound of hard working twin Napier's carries on the chill wind of the autumn morning.

A mile south of the station we pass Selkirk branch junction and the remains of the line to the county town of Selkirkshire an area famous for shoe making and the making of tweeds and tartans. Folk from the town have long been known as 'Souters' meaning shoe makers. With the gradients much easier we climb at 60mph towards the town of Melrose and its superb station and Abbey (reputed to be the resting place of some of the remains of Robert the Bruce) Running on 60 foot jointed track the clickty-clack sound is broken for a moment by Ravenswood Junction and another one time Borders line to Duns.

After flashing through St Boswells at 65mph we pass the recently closed line to Kelso and Tweedmouth a line which almost certainly was used by Deltics prior to closure and scene of the time diversionary route before its severance as a through line by the almost apocalyptic floods in the summer of 1948. Our driver recounts warmly of how his predecessors would run that way with the nonstop *Capitals Limited* after thrashing their A4 over Falahill to avoid wasting time stopping for a banking engine. These enterprising men were not going to allow a diversion to get in the way of a nonstop trip to London and the tender would be in desperate need of water as they approached the first water troughs at Lucker back on the mainline. As we twist and turn through Sir Walter Scott countryside we pass Belses and Hassendene stations at close to 70mph the Deltic now eating up the miles with ease as the first sitting of lunch was being called in the restaurant car a few coaches behind us. After almost 50 miles of running we encounter our first cautionary signal on the approach to the town of Hawick the brakes go on hard as D9009 glides to a halt with 2 columns of lazy exhaust climbing skywards over the town.

The station at Hawick was situated on a viaduct high over the River Teviot and a visitor today would find it almost impossible to visualise this scene such is the scale of change in the last half a century or more. Our driver is passed a message from the one remaining signal box that we have a light engine running in front of us and as soon as it had cleared the block section ahead we would be on our way. This impromptu stop allowed the driver to nip back into the first coach to answer a call of nature and for a few minutes we are left alone to enjoy the sights and sounds of the footplate. The sliding open of the cab door is followed by a chill blast of wind as Jock returns to his office. The semaphore section signal at the end of the platform finally clears as a tuneless parp on the Deltics horn followed by a brief rise in engine tone signalled the start of the 10 mile climb to the summit at Whitrope.

The start away from Hawick is a tortuous one and careful use of the power handle is needed to keep the amps under control and avoid wheel slip in the damp cutting up the 1:72 gradients towards Lynwood viaduct. The locomotives flanges squealed around the tight curves as more amps are fed into our 6 traction motors. Now hugging the west side of the Slitrig valley speed is held at 30 mph and it is only on the approach to the site of the former army camp at Stobbs is the power handle fully pulled fully open The twin Napier's scream in defiance as we crossed Barnes viaduct and onto the steepest part of the climb at 1:65. Stobbs was once the location of a huge military training camp and had one of the largest signal boxes on the line to control the fans of sidings running into the camp itself.

We continue to climb in a southerly direction and follow the course of the Slitrig water still on a rising gradient of 1:65. The gradient finally eases over the magnificent 15 arch Shankend viaduct and allows our Deltic to gain a little speed before the final slog through the wild and windswept uplands. The valley opens up for the last few miles to Sandy Edge and the 1200 yard long Whitrope Tunnel. The handle remains wide open for the whole length of the tunnel and right up until the line briefly ran level before passing the famous summit box and remote cottages.

55002 pauses at Riccarton Junction with a Farewell tour on January 4th 1969. Almost nothing remains of this scene today.

With the climbing now finished for this leg of the journey it is all downhill for the next 13 miles or so to the English border at Kershopefoot. With speed still limited to 45mph careful and frequent use of the vacuum brake is needed as the long train snakes round the reverse curves towards Riccarton Junction. This totally unique community totally depended on the railways for its existence and with no road access until 1963 everything had to be brought in or out by train, even the local Doctor in Hawick would travel up on a specially commandeered light engine if needed.

We are now heading southwards under the shadow of Arnton Fell and still on a falling gradient of 1:75. The small wayside station at Steele Road flashed by as a short burst of power saw us over the small hump passed the ballast quarry at Mains and onto the magnificent Sandholm Viaduct and the approach to Newcastleton station (scene of the infamous last day protests involving outraged residents led by Reverend Brydon Maybon who at one point was taken briefly into custody by the local police) We are now following the course of the Liddel Water as the train twisted and turned at 60mph ever nearer to the Border City of Carlisle. After a further 2 mile descent this time at 1:200 we pass through Riddings Junction, the junction station for the recently closed Langholm branch and where we would have emerged had the railway had followed its original planned route from Hawick via Langholm.

The gradient continues to fall as we flew through Scotch Dyke exactly 86.5 miles from Edinburgh. We are now deep in the debatable lands and our driver tells us tales of the murderous 16th century feuds between Border families such as the Hetherington's, Ormiston's, Armstrongs, Grahams and such like.

The last major centre of note is Longtown with its town on the east side of the river Esk and the station on the west. It is now virtually level all the way to Carlisle and after clearing a 20mph engineering slack on the towns level crossing our Deltic is opened up to clear its throat and accelerate its train up to 70mph the ruling line speed for the remaining 10 miles. Lynside and Harker stations pass by at speed along with the small wayside halt at Parkhouse built to serve the large military and munitions presence in the area. In fact Parkhouse would continue to see a daily workers DMU service for some time after the line had closed as a through route.

The brakes now came on hard for the climb over the WCML at Kingmoor and onto the Eden Viaduct. With flanges squealing in protest and made our final approach to Carlisle passed the five story Canal box, with the former junction for the Silloth branch trailing in from the right. Finally we rumble over Port Carlisle Junction and into Citadel station. We arrive at our journeys end in platform 4 a few minutes over 2 hours and 30 minutes since leaving the Scottish capital. Carlisle was once home to no fewer than 7 railway companies and its station stands between the Citadel (prison and court house in the same building, very convenient) from which it gets its name. We thanks Jock for his hospitality and jump down onto the platform to allow the relieving Newcastle crew access to the cab for the next leg over the 60 mile Tyne Valley route to Newcastle.

Walking past the impressive bulk of an idling **ALYCIDON** we climb into the train to undertake the final leg of our journey to Newcastle by the more conventional means of a BR mark 1 coach.

D9009 ALYCIDON prepares to depart from Edinburgh with the 1330 Heart of Midlothian service in this undated 1960's image.

Deltics on Merseyside pictorial by Pete Chambers

55015 Tulyar, 2040 to York 22/10/81. Copyright Pete Chambers

55008 The Green Howards at Lime Street before working the 13:05 to York. Copyright Pete Chambers.

55022 stands beside an 81 with a Grand National race day special at Liverpool in March 1980. Copyright Pete Chambers.

55002 KOYLI is seen a few minutes before departure with the 20:40 Liverpool to York service. Pete Chambers.

Richie Brown gallery

55012 CREPELLO passes York TMD whilst working 1S76 on 17/6/80. Copyright Richie Brown.

55016 GORDON HIGHLANDER has its boiler tested in the Barn at York TMD on 20/9/80 Copyright Richie Brown

Chapter 5

Working with Deltics

As a former footplate man, the manning of Deltic hauled services is a subject that has always fascinated me. The crewing arrangements were far more complex a matter than the casual observer may think in an industry that is heavily unionised and a lot of money was to be made by those with Deltics on their traction card. With such a small fleet predominantly deployed on the ECML, the number of drivers at each depot trained on the class was closely controlled. With the type of work they were employed on being the prestigious top link services then a very strict pecking order of whom was trained and when was strictly adhered to. In addition to all the local agreements and codifications, each region had a manning committee made up of management and staff side representatives, who would in essence oversee depot workloads, implement national manning agreements and also strictly control spheres of influence over the route and traction knowledge each depot had.

To rail enthusiasts and other interested observers the Deltic locomotives stood head and shoulders amongst all other classes of their time. However this was not always the case for those who had to work on the class day in and day out. I remember as a young man undertaking MP12 driver training at Haymarket in 1985, how many of the staff I spoke to about the passing of the class only a few shorts years before shocked me with the complete apathy they felt towards the king of the diesels. In fact some footplate men even went as far as to tell me they would often fail a Deltic for traffic with some minor defect when it was the only class member on shed knowing full well they would be given a class 47/4 as a replacement, not what I was expecting at all. Whilst the 47 would have less power it had a more driver friendly cab and forwards visibility from the large windscreen was superior to the smaller curved windscreen of a 55. Plus of course the booming of twin Napier's a few feet behind the driver would be removed if a 47 was used instead. Time loss in Scotland even with the 12 or 13 coaches of a named express train would be negligible and what happened beyond Newcastle with the 95mph top speed of the 47 was no concern of the Haymarket man. Selfish I know but a symptom of how the industry was back then, but then again towards the end of a whole week of Newcastle jobs and following over 1000 miles in the cabs of these locomotives but we can forgive ever so slightly such behaviour.

So let's start by taking a look at the depots that drove our favourite class of locomotive on a regular basis and the routes they covered. My former depot of Haymarket only had booked work to/from Newcastle as all other destinations in Scotland saw workings on only an ad-hoc basis. With low line speeds the top speed of 100mph was rarely achieved north of the border although the power of all those horses would have been appreciated when recovering from delays. Haymarket men did of course get to drive over the Waverley route before its closure in 1969, to/from Perth, Aberdeen, Carstairs and Glasgow. All of these with the exception of the summer dated 0910 Dundee to Kings Cross were on trains not booked to be hauled by a 55.

The structure at Haymarket was made of 5 links all of which contained drivers trained on Deltic locomotives. All links had Newcastle work within them but only links 1-3 signed the route to Aberdeen. Number 4 link was the former Waverley route passenger and number 5 the goods link. These links also contained much of the non-mileage payment and therefore second tier work to Carstairs, Glasgow and Perth were scattered throughout each link. A little known fact is that towards the end of the locomotives lives that machines were occasionally put on Carstairs turns just to maintain driver traction knowledge as more and more HST diagram's took away regular daytime Deltic driving to Newcastle The ex Dalry Road men signed Carlisle via the WCML and the ex-Leith Central men had all of the DMU knowledge. Dalry Road (64C) shed closed in 1963 with drivers transferring to Haymarket or taking redundancy from the industry. Leith Central (64H) was the home of the Edinburgh rail car fleet and closed its doors for the last time in April 1972 once the rail cars transferred to Haymarket and their new home in the infamous and smoky east sidings with all units stabled outdoors in what were known to staff as the battery end roads by virtue of battery charging equipment always being present due to the unreliability of the start batteries fitted to the DMU units along with the huge amount of TLC these elderly machines needed just to limp through another days work. Another unusual fact in regard to Haymarket drivers is they always booked on/off on the shed. Any 64B driver on a Deltic hauled service would bring his own engine off the shed or return one to the shed at the end of a day's work. This made a Newcastle mileage turn up to 256 miles when associated engine moves were added. No stepping on/off at the mainline station for the men at this depot unlike their peers further south.

In the twilight of the locomotives lives, some variations to the work undertaken at Haymarket resulted in strange events such as a Driver and Drivers Assistant being paired up with a Millerhill freight guard to work the 0048 Edinburgh to Newcastle sleeper train before returning north to the now closed freightliner terminal at Portobello with a liner train running via the also now closed spur via Wanton Walls. Another Deltic hauled job was the 1707 stopping service to Newcastle. The roster for this turn showed it being crewed by 2 drivers A+B and a Drivers Assistant C. the reason for this strange apparent overmanning was down to the need to have 2 drivers on the return HST service from Newcastle with the DA travelling home passenger as they were now not needed due to the steam heating and coupling duties on 1E29 completed. Four members of train crew if you include the guard and a 3300hp type 5 diesel locomotive making it one would assume a very uneconomic working indeed. Another anomaly involving Haymarket based drivers would take place on as a consequence of the frequent visit of the class to Aberdeen with 1S12 the 0550 ex London. This turn was in fact worked by a Ferryhill driver from Aberdeen north of Edinburgh. Drivers from this depot as you will know did not have traction knowledge for the mighty Deltic. When there was no other traction with air brakes or electric train heating available then a juggle of drivers would be needed to get the Haymarket man onto 1S12. From memory the Edinburgh man who was booked to work the 0710 Leeds to Aberdeen forwards would be held back for 1S12 with the Aberdeen man who should have worked 1S12 being sent home passenger after coming south earlier that morning with the 0855 Aberdeen to Kings Cross. The complexities of driver training also came into the equation as the Scottish Region stopped driver training on Deltics relatively early in comparison to the Eastern Region. Drivers Bob Tierney and Harry Cooper were trained in 1977 after which no further training took place. Anyone arriving at the depot after 1978 would have been placed in either the DMU only Link 5 or would not have been able to work on a Deltic hauled service without a conductor driver.

Of course on a more positive note Haymarket men had an involvement with the class from the arrival of the prototype Deltic in 1958 which arrived via the Waverley route driven by   Bill Nairn who had been given special tuition on the locomotive to bring it up from Carlisle and to drive it on road tests on the ECML to Berwick upon Tweed and also on the Aberdeen road. Another 64B driver Dave Duncan had the honour of working out of Edinburgh on June 16th 1962 with an immaculate D9000 following its naming ceremony prior to departure with the 10 o'clock *Flying Scotsman* to Kings Cross. How fitting if a 64B driver should be in charge of the first arrival in the country that another Haymarket men should work the last passenger departure from Scotland on January 2nd 1982 when passed driver Ian Royall brought **ROYAL SCOTS GREY** off Haymarket TMD for the very last time and onto the Deltic Scotsman Farewell for its final ever run south under British Rail ownership. Although in the interests of accuracy 55015 crewed by Gateshead men did follow behind light engine to York and **TULYAR** was therefore the last Deltic to cross the border as the curtain finally came down on the first mainline era of this remarkable class.

A footnote about the early cessation of driver training in Scotland compared to the NER who still trained on Deltics until 1979 and the ER who carried on until the summer of 1980 makes one wonder if some embryonic plans existed to transfer the locomotives away from Scotland much earlier than was the ultimate reality as I cannot fathom out why training would cease in 1977 when the planned withdrawal date for the class was still at this time in the 1982-1984 range. Something must have been behind that decision and I would dearly love to know what it was as the training course itself was only 5 days long so could hardly be classed as a financial burden on the region. I can only assume that early plans must have existed for the class to no longer visit Scotland when the full roll out of HST's had taken place but of course this is only my opinion and the reason if one exists falls very firmly into the railway X files.

Gateshead drivers had work along the length of the whole ECML with turns between Newcastle and Edinburgh along with jobs to York, Doncaster and even London itself. Gateshead was one of the 2 depots in the diesel era to work the prestigious non-stop services between Tyne side and the capital city. London based drivers doing similar work albeit in reverse. These working involved crews lodging overnight in either London or Newcastle before coming out of lodge the next day for the homewards working.

These were just the types of workings the locomotives were built for, 268 miles of non-stop running with 400 tons plus on the drawbar. I am told by those who used to work such turns that Deltics would cruise for mile after mile at 100mph and as you would expect have power in reserve should late running or other out of course delays impact on time keeping. More junior footplate men who would have prepared the locomotives for these top link jobs must have felt more than a twinge of envy as they handed over control to their senior colleagues no doubt carrying both a kit bag and overnight bag. The *Flying Scotsman* and *Talisman* were the trains shared between these men of the iron road as both services ran non-stop London to Newcastle or in the case of the *Talisman* to Darlington. I am led to believe by another former boss of mine Alistair Smith that the crew who worked north with the *Flying Scotsman* on a Monday came south on Tuesday with the up working. The Gateshead drivers worked up with the *Talisman* before returning home with the *Flying Scotsman* the next day. These double lodge turns gave crews 2 nights away per week before an extended period of rest days. Newcastle based drivers did of course did more than just London work. They shared the Edinburgh expresses with Haymarket men. Later on they worked over the Tyne Valley to Carlisle following the extension of the 0718 ex Edinburgh through to the Border city in the winter timetable change of 1980. Before that they worked diverted Anglo Scots during the Penmanshiel block and before that on a more ad-hoc basis from almost the classes' introduction in the 1960's. In fact this one was one of the routes used by Newcastle drivers for driver training with both empty coaching stock and a summer dated Newcastle to Ayr service being used with the Deltic being removed from the train at Carlisle. Throughout the whole of the life of daily Deltic operation, footplate staff was governed by a fixed working day of 8 hours. This restriction which was only altered by the long and protracted flexible rostering strike of 1982 placed limits on how far Gateshead drivers could work when on non-lodging turns. Newcastle to Doncaster and back was a favourite Deltic job as was Newcastle to York on overnight services as the less frequent train service and slacker 90mph schedules prevented going further afield. Although right up to at least 1980 the famous centre road crew changes at Doncaster were a daily event with for an example a Doncaster crew brining the *Night Aberdonian* down from London before a Newcastle crew would work forwards to Tyneside after coming up with the 2100 passenger and mail train which was booked to be Deltic hauled at various times over the life of the class.

Top link drivers at York tended to work the slower services which stopped at York for a crew change and then onwards to London with a small number of stops. They also worked the well-known Stockport mail service over the Pennines via Stalybridge. I remember the 1550 stopping service to London was crewed from York as was the 0805 service in the morning. The return working for the latter was the 1S60 overnight to Aberdeen. The York driver working ex London was relieved by another York man to Newcastle for a Haymarket man to Edinburgh for another Haymarket man forwards to Aberdeen. The return working for 1A08 was the 1220 service arriving in York just after 1500. It was only really following the transfer of all the non-London based locomotives to York in 1979 did 50A drivers really begin to build up a reputation as hard hitters with the class.

Doncaster drivers also enjoyed a wide variety of destinations on their route cards. This resulted in them driving Deltics to Newcastle, Leeds, and Hull plus of course London. In the twilight of the locomotives career, both the up and down *Hull Executive*'s were worked by Doncaster men including the short lived 91 minute sprint from Kings Cross to Retford. It was through this working that many of them became legends to those interested in timing such workings; names that are still in the memory include Jim Robertson and Joe Hodgson, both drivers knew what their right hand was capable of as they wrung every last ounce of power from a late running Deltic.

Leeds Holbeck was another location which enjoyed some prestigious Deltic workings with the London Executive and Pullman trains been driven by men from this depot. Liverpool Lime Street, Bradford and

Harrogate were all on the route cards of Holbeck men. The knowledge of drivers from this depot allowed Deltics to wander off the beaten track, as we have already seen in earlier chapters. Visits along the Calder Valley line, Settle and Carlisle, Bradford Forster Square and of course Blackpool would all have involved a Deltic trained Holbeck man. With the notable exception of some of the fast West Riding to London trains these drivers may not have made the name for themselves that others did but this was more than compensated with the variety of work such a large route card could bring.

With Gateshead men now in charge, the 08:00 down service awaits departure from York with 9006 in charge.

Further south a few drivers till remained at Grantham possibly as a legacy from when steam locomotives used to be changed over here. This small but useful group of men were responsible for the odd Deltic working to Skegness and also allowed either of the 2 Grantham commuter trains to be Deltic hauled should a locomotive happen to fall onto the diagram.

Peterborough drivers had regular Deltic work on both the Cleethorpes jobs and also the commuter services to/from London which admittedly were not booked for Deltic haulage but could and did produce on at least a weekly basis. Diverted Anglo Scots would also feature drivers from this location. The Joint Line via Lincoln to Doncaster and also the long way round to London March' Cambridge would often have 'Bungits' acting route conductors to Deltic drivers from further afield.

55008 THE GREEN HOWARDS working 1S72. Copyright Richie Brown

With Kings Cross men ex lodge on board.9001 ST PADDY gets ready to depart with 1E05 the up Flying Scotsman nonstop

55019 Royal Highland Fusilier takes a breather and a crew change at Newcastle with the 15:00 ex Kings Cross bound for Edinburgh.

A rolled up newspaper is used to assist in backing 9011 into platform 7 ready for another run north in May 1973.

At last but not least London men (no women on footplate back then so not a derogatory term) In many people's eyes these were the elite of the footplate fraternity when it came to the type of Deltic hauled services driven and also the wide route knowledge the complex link structure would have. Newcastle, Leeds, Cleethorpes along with several smaller places in between. Kings Cross drivers worked the prestigious *Flying Scotsman* the *Leeds Executive* and also the *Talisman* and before that the *Elizabethan* many barnstorming performance can be credited to London based drivers as can many of the early test trains along with prestigious events such as the *Centenary Scotsman*, inaugural *Silver Jubilee* plus of course the *Talisman* and *Flying Scotsman*.

Richards story- (1998/2003)

By the spring of 1998 following the privatisation of ICWC the previous year my new employer Virgin decided in their wisdom to move my job from London to its HQ in Birmingham. This resulted in a house move to Shrewsbury and placed me in the ideal location to be one of the volunteers to be trained on **ROYAL SCOTS GREY** ready for its use on XC services over the summer. So on a sunny Thursday morning, Saltley driver Brian Harper and I travelled to Stewarts Lane in South London to be given the necessary instruction by John Wardle and Chris Wayman. As the locomotive would only ever operate on Virgins safety case with a travelling fitter then our training was of a more practical nature. So the day spent on the loco covered,

- Preparing the locomotive for service along with all of the safety checks of consumables, brakes and warning horns and safety equipment needed before leaving a depot. This did of course include the golden rule of always starting the power unit furthest away from you first.
- Driving technique on the mainline as obviously the locomotive handled very differently to any other type and overloading the traction motors especially when starting away was an easy if avoidable mistake to make. In addition buffering up to coaching stock could also be a challenge as if anything other than a cautious approach was taken then the Deltic would bounce off the stock or in the worst case push the coaching stock back into the buffers even with all brakes applied.
- Last but not least disposal of the locomotive at the end of the working day to ensure it was safely secured had all lighting extinguished to prevent flat batteries and in the preservation era was locked to prevent unauthorised access.

- With a travelling fitter on board, either the legendary Chris Wayman or the genial Mike Garrigan we only needed limited training on fault finding not that RSG failed that often but a couple of close shaves took place whilst on the Ramsgate's almost resulted in the locomotive being removed from the up train at Rugby on one occasion and requiring assistance from Didcot on another return trip.

After driving RSG light engine back to Birmingham the next day we were both signed off as competent and my professional relationship with D9000 began. Over the next 2 years I was fortunate enough to work with RSG to Carlisle, Reading and on at least 8 occasions Ramsgate. The latter trips would involve booking on at 0445 book at Oxley depot to prepare the locomotive before running light engine to New Street via Bescot and Soho. The stock arrived in New Street 47 hauled from Derby and with a departure of 0658 there was little time for hanging about and more often than not D9000 would only be coupled to the stock with minimum time available for a brake test and paperwork handover before departure. Not that station staff minded as concerns were always being raised about RSG setting off the station fire alarms and in fact a instruction was issued that the ECS had to be positioned in such a way that the Deltics exhausts were well outside the station canopy. New Street station was meant to have extraction fans to dissipate fumes from various diesel classes including HST's. However I don't ever remember them being effective enough to deal with all that RSG chucked out.

We would run out via the WCML before picking up the Hither Green conductor driver at Kensington Olympia before heading into the complex suburban network of south London. The normal route would see us run via Herne Hill, Bromley South, Chatham and Margate. On the return D9000 would retrace its steps but run via Bromley South, Peckham Rye, Kenny O and then onto the Western via Acton Wells Junction. After a slow line stagger to Reading it was then more often than not a fast run home via Didcot, Oxford and the scenic Cherwell Valley to Banbury and Leamington Spa. The WCML would be re-joined at Coventry before a final 100mph sprint into Birmingham NS. After RSG was uncoupled from 1S87 we would take the long route back to Oxley via Lifford Curve, Saltley, and Saltley LIP for fuel and then home to bed via Sutton Park and Walsall.

My final run out with the Deltic was from Wolverhampton to Plymouth on January 20th 1999, when after some unsavoury and childish scenes regarding who got to drive the locomotive along the sea wall I decided enough was enough and on the following Monday took my name off the list of staff who could be used on such workings. One driver's ego had got in the way of professionalism and I remember sitting alone on the footplate at Plymouth wondering how we were going to get the train back to Birmingham without another tantrum breaking out. Ironically the young Exeter driver who's older colleague thought incompetent of driving RSG put in an exemplary performance back to Bristol and I believe demolished several of the RPS long standing best times for the route. I had a simple philosophy on these trips and that was everyone who could drive got the opportunity to do so for at least a small part of the trip. The same principle applied to cab guests and we never refused an approved cab ride unless difficult events on the footplate such as the day we ran between Cholsey and Didcot with both engines shut down due to high water temperature and it being touch and go if forwards momentum would get us over the junction and clear of the SWML prevented it. On another occasion an enthusiast and his young son came up to me upset that their reserved seats in the leading coach had been taken by someone who was refusing to move. I found them another seat on the train and by way of an apology I arranged for them to occupy the best seat in the house with a cab ride from Reading to Oxford. If they are DPS members then I hope they remember the day as the look on the little lads face was a picture of sheer joy as the cab door was slid open for them to hop aboard and to join Saltley seagull Tim Wattison up front.

The whole experience of Plymouth once again diminished my love affair with Deltic Locomotives and to be frank it certainly galvanised my belief that work and hobbies don't mix. It would be a long time before I went near the cab of a Deltic hauled train again. Nothing could not have been further from my mind when one Wednesday afternoon I received a phone call which went something like- Didn't you used to be an Inverness driver -Answer yes, don't you have traction knowledge of Deltics, answer again yes. So that's how I came to be involved in the Deltic Freedom of Scotland, without doubt one of the highlights of my professional career and a never to be forgotten opportunity to help 9 and 19 operate successfully over my old haunts and past my childhood home in Muir of Ord. I don't have much love for the modern rail industry, but without doubt this trip would not have happened under a state owned railway so for the ability to operate the Deltic FOS I thank John Major and his Tory chums along with of course all those who spent hours of their time arranging it and making it the best rail tour ever.

Brian Harper, Chris Wayman and the author alight from D9000 on Saltley after another days work is over.

Even the authors wife Jane has grown to love the majestic class 55's

Richie Brown story- (1978/82)

My grandparents lived just 50 yards from the East Coast Main Line and so I was introduced to the sights and sounds of Deltics at an early age. Their house was just off Leeman Road in York, my grandfather was a retired railwayman. So it wasn't much of a surprise that I wanted to work on the footplate.

I started as a Driver's Assistant at Doncaster Depot in 1978 and after 18 months of traveling from my home in York I got a transfer back home to the Depot on Leeman Road. I was lucky enough to work on 18 out of the 22 Deltics.

At Doncaster, the Top link went London and Newcastle, No 2 and 3 links went to London (as well as many other routes). The top two links also signed via Gainsborough and Sleaford but as far as I know they didn't sign the Hertford diversionary route.

We had a few tea time and early evening turns to London as we were needed for the steam-heating on return workings, as well as some early morning turns taking the overnights into Kings Cross.

We did the "W" shunt off Kings Cross Loco to get the locomotive to the other side of the station, this involved the driver staying at the North facing cab and I would be in the South facing cab. Once you were in Gasworks Tunnel and behind the signal I would apply the straight air brake, then when the signal cleared I would release the brake and sound the horn, the driver would then apply power and we would go into one of the mid-platforms and once behind the platform signal, we would repeat the move into Gasworks Tunnel again to get to the far side of the station, this was usually for 1S70 the 2215 *Night Aberdonian* which would have a load of 15 vehicles. I once asked why wasn't it called the "M" shunt (the top two points of the letter M representing Gasworks Tunnel) and the Driver I was with replied "Don't be stupid young 'un" (so I never did find out). When I transferred to York Depot in mid 1979 I would never do that shunt again as York Drivers didn't sign KX Loco plus in May of the same year the passenger loco closed for ever.

Some of the overnight trains got relief in the centre roads at Doncaster, a practice which has long since disappeared, much like the trains themselves. As we would pull up to the signal on the fast, you would see the light of a bardic lamp on the ground and there would be your relief. On northbound services I would often ask for a lift home to York, this way I got to know some of the Gateshead crews. One thing I picked up from most drivers at various depots was the respect they had for Deltics. I was often told "they're noisy, they're draughty" but they also seemed to agree that they would get you home if you looked after them properly.

I was on a job from Doncaster to Newcastle one night and after leaving York - where the Driver had to position the locomotive so that we could top up the water tanks for the boiler (this was usually on Platform 14 as it was then numbered). As we progressed north, my driver told me about an incident he was involved in the year before. He was on 55 008 on Feb 16th 1977 on a daytime Newcastle job and as he started braking for the stop at Darlington he realised something was seriously wrong. Even though the train brake pipe was reducing (meaning that brakes would be applying on all the passenger coaches) only the brakes on the locomotive were being applied. He described how he took the 40 mph points off the main line at "well over 60", he described how 55008 rocked from side to side as he shot into Darlington station with the horn blaring. The train didn't stop until it came out of the north end of the station and collided with a DMU coming into the station as ECS, the train continued onto the line to Bishop Auckland, before finally being stopped by the guard pulling the emergency chain. Apparently what had happened was on his way between York and Darlington a "foreign object" had bounced up between the loco and the first carriage, isolating the train brakes, which is why these days all brake handles have a catch on them so it cannot happen again. So, I asked him if he had been worried, he looked at me and replied "I knew I was safe in the old girl". Then as we approached Darlington, he suddenly shouted "Oh no it's happening again!" Then he started laughing and said "Just look at your face!!" Needless to say we had an uneventful journey.

On another night turn to Newcastle, the boiler fault light came on near Thirsk and as it was a bitterly cold night my driver said I had better get that sorted out. He said he would ease off for 5 minutes to reduce the noise in the engine room. When I went back it seemed to be a simple job to get the boiler working again and soon returned to the cab. No sooner had I sat down that the fault light came back on "You better fix it properly this time" my mate muttered "and I'm not shutting off the power as I don't want to be late", so ear defenders on back I went to tinker about with the boiler. I wedged myself against the bodyside as I monitored the boilers performance and after a few minutes it settled down and remained working, it was then that I realised we were pulling into Darlington station, so I opened one of the engine room windows and stuck my head out, enjoying the fresh air. The look on a couple of Royal Mail staff was priceless as we rolled by.

At the time, you got paid extra for "mileage" turns (over 200 miles in a shift) and as Doncaster to Kings Cross was 156 miles, a two-way job was paid extra. With the high number of overnight services requiring a Drivers Assistant it was not unusual to get four KX jobs in a single week, this had the sometimes uncomfortable result that as a teenager I would sometimes earn more than a Driver in one of the lower links.

When I got my transfer to York Depot there were a lot less jobs to Kings Cross. We had one turn which was actually booked for two drivers and a Drivers Assistant (because of the limit at the time of 175 miles one-way single manned) We worked the 1550 York -KX (1A26) and back with the 2000 off KX (1S60), which was steam-heated and was the reason why we were required on the job.

The 1550 departure time of 1A26 meant that we would parallel the 1550 departure to Liverpool (1M76) out of York. On more than one occasion the Liverpool would beat us under Holgate Bridge, but by the time we passed Dringhouses we would be ahead, once the second field-divert kicked in the power just seemed to keep coming. One driver said to me "These Deltics may be a bit steady when you start them rolling but once they get going they just keep going on and on, much like my wife when she starts talking!"

With GD and HA locomotives transferred to York it was not surprising that we dealt with a lot of Deltics on the various shed turns. One evening my Driver was busy playing dominoes and when we had a loco to move he asked if I had my own key, when I nodded my head, he told me to "get on with the job and don't mess it up", the foreman told us "to drag a 47 off the fuel point and use 55017 as that needed to be put in B Group sidings as well" I was well pleased as I always liked the GD machines above the others. After completing the job and shutting down 55017 I walked back into the newsroom feeling quite proud of myself and at that point told my driver "You know the Deltic is alright to do shed shunts with" at which point he burst out laughing and accused me of being "of a low IQ and my parents weren't married". Okay he had a point I mean the visibility wasn't that great for shunting and you had to be careful with the power handle! BUT I was still feeling pleased with myself! However it wasn't the only time I raised a good laugh. The very next night, with the same driver, we were asked to bring 55 011 out of No1 Road and onto the fuelling point. He looked at me and gave me a wink "You can manage that on your own"... I walked through the shed and the fitters had started one of the engines. I climbed aboard and took the parking brake off, gave a short blast of the horn and proceeded to fuelling point some 100 yards ahead. As I came out of the shed building and onto the point, my driver along with foreman and the fitter were stood there clapping and laughing! I had assumed when I found 55011 running that fitters had completed everything and I didn't do a walk-round check and as a result I had dragged a battery charger the full length of No 1 road still attached to 55011. I can laugh about it now and I learned my lesson as I never did anything like it again up to my retirement 37 years later.

Before "flexible rostering" was introduced all driving turns were 8 hours, apart from one turn we had at York which was 10 hours (0715 to 1715) this was the Crewe Loco Ferry turn, this was manned by a link with just three drivers in it and they were all ex top link men who had terrific route and traction knowledge. There were three drivers as they also covered the 1000 Derby Loco Ferry turn. These turns didn't run every day to Crewe, sometimes you would collect a locomotive or two from another depot (Gateshead for example) and then the next day take them to Crewe. I used to swap for this turn as it was always different and I often took my camera. However, one day in January 1980 I didn't take my camera as the weather was lousy. Booking on at 0715, I met one of the regular drivers Eric Pearson, who was a true gentleman (and introduced me to drinking Bovril) and a second driver from the same link Tommy Crowe, so I knew new were dragging locomotives as you needed a "rider" as well as a DA if we dragged more than one loco. We had a Brush 4 (class 47) and a whistler (class 40) to take to Crewe. The foreman had a smile on his face and said to Eric "Make sure you bring it back we need it tonight and it's only running on one engine" My ears pricked up at this point! It couldn't be? BUT yes we had 55 014 (another favoured GD machine) as our loco. Before the days of internet and mobile phones etc… nobody got to know about what we had that day, our journey across the pennines was uneventful. At the time Deltics were almost regular performers on the Liverpool route but I don't think many made it to Crewe! As we arrived onto Crewe Diesel Depot I will never forget the foreman who came out of his office rather sharply and shouted up "You're not leaving that here, take it back where you came from!" which after refilling our tea-cans we did!

Sometimes Deltics made it to Stockport on the York-Shrewsbury TPO, as York men, we only took the train to Leeds and then waited the time it took for the Leeds men to go to Stockport and back before returning the train to York. Not the most productive of shifts, but at the time depots were protective of their route knowledge and Leeds men were already not happy with York drivers working to Liverpool. One night we had a Deltic on the train from York and my Driver said "You might as well have a go son", I wasn't going to say No was I? I gingerly departed York on time and we made our way to Leeds. By the time we got to Church Fenton we were a few minutes late due to temporary speed restrictions in place. I found out how much power the Deltics had as we stormed up the bank to Micklefield, I was a bit generous with the power handle and managed to wheel spin at 60mph more than once before topping the bank at 70mph and we made an on-time arrival at Leeds. As we walked back along the train towards the messroom one of the doors of the TPO slid open and one of the Royal Mail staff leaned out for a smoke….he looked up as we passed "Bit of a vigorous run tonight Driver" he muttered.

Due to a number of factors including the introduction of HST's and the training of drivers on this new traction and the increased use of Deltics on Liverpool turns, at York Depot, Drivers were still being trained on Deltics in 1980! Sometimes this would mean that drivers who may have had 30 plus years experience were being trained on new traction. One morning I was in the mess room at the depot as the empty coaching stock from Clifton was being brought into the station for the 0805 departure to KX. It was a winter's morning and there is a slight incline from the shunt release line at Clifton. We heard the drone of a Deltic as it slowly approached the depot. Unfortunately whoever was driving had the power handle open too far and the engines kept overloading with an audible "thud", followed by a resurgence of power and this cycle would repeat itself as it approached. By the time it passed the depot there must have been a handful of drivers along with a few DAs looking out of the window. One of the top link men was stood there and muttered about "that's the trouble putting these young 'uns on a proper loco".

I did manage to have a few shifts with a top link man who knew his stuff Harry "odd socks" Wilson. He was a quiet man who was always happy to share his knowledge with us DAs. We didn't work with regular mates and so it was a "good day" when I would see I was with Harry. He put me in the seat one day on the 1550 York - London KX and he was happy to sit on the right-hand seat for the journey to Doncaster (where another driver would be joining us) as we approached Selby I wasn't too sure where the 80mph restriction started. But Harry was laid back and he just looked over to me and said "I normally do 80 from this bridge" as I passed it doing about 90, he smiled and told me that "we all have to learn". He said "You're still taking it Doncaster tho'". It was many years later that I remembered how laid back he appeared BUT he knew exactly where we were and allowed me to learn without being too domineering and I tried to do the same with new Drivers that were learning with me.

Not all top link drivers were as friendly. There had been quite a gap in recruitment at York Depot and there were some DAs at York with 15 plus years service, so I was a "new boy" to some, and also a different generation. I heard tales from some of the old boys who were firemen to my great-grandfather when they started, apparently he treated some of them in quite an off-hand manner (to put it mildly) I was working with one "old school" driver into London Kings Cross who was moaning about the state of some of the KX men, he was wearing full uniform including shirt and tie and cap whilst many KX drivers didn't, some were even wearing jeans and they were younger as well! So I wasn't exactly looking forward to being with him all the way back to York on the 2000 departure (1S60). This train wasn't usually a Deltic but this evening we had a Deltic as our "office" home. I wasn't bothered if the Driver wasn't going to talk to me as I still enjoyed the experience of being in the cab of such a machine on a run from Kings Cross to York. We departed on time and all was going well until we passed Potters Bar when there was a loud bang sound behind us. We continued and as were approached Welwyn Garden City we were routed onto the platform (which was unusual) as we ran through the platform two staff started waving at us, so of course I waved back! But as we passed them they appeared to be pointing behind us, so my driver opened the window and looked back "oh oh" he said and looked at me "we might have a fire…BUT I don't want to stop, I want to get back home. See what you can do" Great I thought, and put my smock on and my ear defenders (most York DAs had them as the boilers located in-between the engines made for a noisy environment if you had to go and check it out). I went into the engine room and there was a bit of black smoke and It looked like some of the exhaust cladding had caught fire. It wasn't that much and looked a lot worse than it really was. After 10-15 minutes and the use of one extinguisher, it seemed like it would be okay. I returned to the cab, drawing back the curtain and stepping up onto my seat. The driver looked across and I told him "we should be okay" and he nodded and then said "Maybe some of you young lads will be alright".

Looking back now to events nearly forty years ago, what strikes me is how quick it seems the Deltics were removed from service. I was aware that changes were on the way. But I had been brought up with the sound of twin Napier engines in the background, I had worked with them for three and a half years and I guess I thought they would always be around, and then just like that they were gone! Since then I have worked on more powerful locomotives however nothing ever seemed to match the Deltics as they not only sounded powerful they also looked powerful as well. Happy Days…

Richie Brown then and now. Copyright Richie Brown.

Paul Nash story- (1964/82)

I had the pleasure of meeting Paul Nash in York on May 23rd 2017 and was immediately struck by his warmth, humour and razor sharp memory in regard to his 17 years spent working on Deltics from 1964-1981. He is one of the few who can claim to have worked these locomotives from Green livery and vacuum brakes only, through Blue livery and non ETH, then duel braked/ETH in blue, white cabs and finally to the bitter end and withdrawal.

Paul started his footplate career in 1960 at March depot in Cambridgeshire. However, as Dr Beeching and his reshaping of Britain's railways report began to bite, he was made redundant and moved to Kings Cross under a 14a priority move and in his own words never looked back.

Pauls previous years of service ensured he went straight into link 3 at his new depot and would work Deltics to Doncaster, and Cambridge on the odd occasion that one would be found on one of the Cambridge Buffet services.

With the end of steam on the Eastern Region promotion for certain grades was fairly rapid and Paul jumped straight from Link 3 to the top link 1 and onto the prestigious and financially lucrative Newcastle lodge jobs. This link could also catch Leeds work when spare. So Paul and his driver would work down to Leeds one day and back the next after lodging in the engineman's hostel at Farnley. Paul remembers lodging here as not an unpleasant experience especially with the right driver but he does describe the hostel itself as somewhat basic and only suitable for a few hours' sleep before booking on duty the next day to return home to the capital. Paul worked many Deltic hauled trains including the prestigious *Queen of Scots Pullman* into Leeds Central before its closure in 1967, and then Leeds City thereafter with the Yorkshire Pullmans and other West Riding trains. The London based locomotives often worked on the Leeds/Bradford road and this is where Paul first worked on his own favourite Deltic which was D9003 **MELD**.

Unlike Leeds the Newcastle lodge was in a hotel at either the Tyne or Westmoreland Hotels situated in the City Centre. London men had the following Newcastle lodges,

- 0100 sleepers down and back 2245 the same day. This was unusual in itself as footplate men rarely if ever booked on twice in the same 24-hour period.
- 1600 T*alisman* down and back next day with the morning *Talisman.*
- 1700 Pullman down and back with the 0745 business train next day.
- London to Edinburgh Freightliner down and back next day with the *Flying Scotsman.*

Gateshead drivers shared the balance of such workings and would as an example lodge in London off the afternoon *Talisman* for the next morning's 10 o'clock or *Flying Scotsman* to the general public.

It was on such working that Paul perhaps uniquely for a passed fireman obtained a driving turn to Newcastle when one Saturday night a colleague failed to take duty and Paul as the night ferry driver ended up working the 2230 sleepers to Newcastle with no notice and without food or shaving tackle. Normally lodge drivers would get a pack of sandwiches known as an Ilford box and then either an evening meal or breakfast once in lodge but never both. So on this night a single sandwich box (or pack up to KX men) had to be shared between driver and his fireman John Hutton.

In the early days of Pauls career the Deltics were of course still operating as vacuum brake and steam heating only machines and he remembers the pure vacuum brake as being a joy to use and a very effective means of stopping even from 90+. He also confirms something I have long suspected which is that when working overnight trains, many drivers would shut down the leading engine after completing the 12 mile climb to Potters Bar to ensure a quieter night for the crew and with trains only timed at 65mph no loss in running would take place. This didn't of course apply when late, as on my trip behind 55021 described earlier when both engines would be kept running and the locomotive driven hard to make up lost time.

Daytime trains were of course a different matter and with heavy 12/13 coach Anglo Scots only a Deltic could come close to keeping time on the heavily temporary speed restricted mainline and even on the shorter 8 coach Leeds and Newcastle trains a 47 would struggle to maintain schedules on anything other than a clear run and if the locomotive was driven absolutely flat out for long periods of time with no margin for recovery from any delay whatsoever.

In talking with Paul, I was struck by the complete lack of diversionary route knowledge Kings Cross men had and other than to Cambridge any deviation from the norm such as the Joint Line or Durham Coast would require the services of a conductor driver. This explains why diverted expresses or night trains would stop at Hitchin or Peterborough as an example to collect or drop off conductor drivers from the smaller depots who did 'sign the road' once away from the mainline. Hitchin drivers would be used for Cambridge diversions, Peterborough for the joint line and so on all the way north. I can imagine it to be a complex logistical operation in arranging but easier as part of a unified network when freight depots could be used at weekends when little freight traffic ran.

Paul became a booked driver on November 21st 1972, after which he went on to drive Deltics and all the other forms of ECML traction right up until his retirement in 1996. In the time we spent together it was obvious that the 55's were held in high regard by most London based drivers and Paul couldn't remember a single complete failure that he was personally involved in with a Deltic although he could of course remember a number of single engine runs especially during the critical power unit shortages of the 1970's. Despite all of these issues Deltics usually got you home along with having vast reserves of power to make up lost time following the numerous delays which could be found on an almost daily basis.

The only criticism he had of Deltics if it can be called that involved the perils of bringing a recently re-blocked locomotive light engine from Finsbury Park to Kings Cross. With the new blocks not yet profiled to the wheels an unwary driver could find himself having insufficient brake force to stop especially at the top end of Clarence Yard where a number of machines including D9000/55022 derailed at the exit signal catch points.

Paul rightly claims to have enough memories of his career to fill the whole book, he has however, asked me to share this one to bring his story to an end. We left Kings Cross one of the night sleepers, Deltic of course as most of them were. My mate Jock Cairns was in the Second man's seat as usual with me driving. He was a very keen music fan was Jock and loved all music.

On this day he had brought a reel to reel tape player to have a few tunes as went on our way. The music he had brought with him was French accordion music.

I knocked the front Engine out when we got over Potters Bar, as we did on most of the Sleepers, nice and quiet. Jock then started the tape and I remember him saying it lasted for 2 hours.

Somewhere between Retford and Doncaster the first side finished 'Turn the light on was the cry, I will turn it over'. I turned the light on and the second reel had failed to pick up the tape and it had been deposited in the foot well of the Deltic.

The Deltic foot well was full and overflowing with recording tape, we were on the race track towards Darlington before he got it back on the reel. Can you imagine the sight of Jock sitting on the floor legs crossed for 2 hours winding the tape back on by hand?

The air was blue, he never brought that tape player to work anymore, what a laugh we had. I still laugh about it today.

Pauls favourite Deltic MELD at the head of a Kings Cross night diagram. Copyright railimagesonline

A drivers running sheet as used by Harry Wilson on 23/7/81. With thanks to Richie Brown.

Chapter 6

Final words

So how did I top events between 1999 and 2003? To be honest I didn't and other than a couple of sociable days out with my wife or friends, I haven't been near a Deltic hauled train since other than a one way trip from York to Tweedbank with **ALYCIDON** in April 2016. However I no longer have the enthusiasm to relive my youth on today's bland railway and my support for the remaining machines is now more of a sedentary one. My focus has shifted towards researching the life and times of our 22 old friends especially in relation to lesser known work they carried out in Scotland particularly over the much missed mainline which used to run passed my home here at Whitrope. With over 1000 photographs and several hundred logs to catalogue, my memoires to write and numerous other bits and bobs to tidy up then I suspect I'm going to be busy for many years yet

In closing I would like to say that I am a firm believer that it's impossible to recreate the past in its entirety and only those who lived through the real Deltic era can claim to have been part of it. The preservation movement does a sterling job in recreating the experience but nothing fires the imagination quite like the down *Flying Scotsman* passing Darlington at speed or a dirty GD regiment humming into York station at 0300 on a long train of sleeping cars. Chasing Deltics was very much part of growing up and reminiscing about them is part of growing old and as for the bit in the middle there is very little if anything I would wish to change.

For some time now, I have thought about producing a definitive list of my most poignant memory of each of the class 55 Deltic locomotives, at last the task is complete. The list is as you would expect personal and based on nothing more than memories from almost 40 years ago.

55001- In July 1977 my family and I were travelling from our home in the Highlands to North Yorkshire. We arrived in Edinburgh, with onward connections to Darlington on the 1755 Edinburgh to Leeds. As we walked down platform 19, I could hear the sound of idling Napier's, **ST PADDY** was standing at the head of the 1700 to Kings Cross, calling at Newcastle and then York. After much pleading, for a change of plan, we boarded the 1700 as far as Newcastle, with a change there for Darlington. **ST PADDY** must have been idling for some time; she cleared her throat on departure, with a thick white exhaust trail which went on and on well past Portobello. The stock for the 1700 was the weekday *Silver Jubilee* rake as each head rest carried one of the white antimacassars specially made for this short lived train. I thoroughly enjoyed my 125 mile ride and even to this day the memory of watching number 1 snaking high above the North Sea and through Berwick stays with me. This turned out to be my one and only run with number 1.

55002- In April 1979 Steve McFarlane and Paul Gildersleve and I travelled south with KOYLI on the 0840 from Leeds. It became quickly obvious that all was not well; No2 kept losing an engine and running for long periods at reduced speed. Whatever the fault was the defective engine would cut back in every 20 miles or so. This caused the strange situation of us running at 80-85 mph and then after returning to full thrust, accelerating up to 107 to win back lost minutes. The net result of all this was a time loss of 20 minutes from Doncaster to London. However, KOYLI epitomised a Gateshead Deltic perfectly that day, filthy, temperamental, noisy and very loveable.

55003- In September 1979, I enjoyed a hugely successful 2 week rail rover on the ECML. Just about every move that I made paid dividends. On the night of September 18th I found myself at Kings Cross covering the North bound overnights. **PINZA** went North on the 2215 to Aberdeen, and **MELD** sat at the head of the 2230 to Edinburgh. I had always had a soft spot for **MELD** ever since my first sighting of her as a very young child, she always seemed to be about, was always clean and now of course had her smart white windows to complete the look. My intent was to travel to Edinburgh with **MELD** and to return south the next morning with the Edinburgh to Plymouth train, which would in all probability be hauled by **PINZA**. On arrival at Peterborough for reasons which even to this day I cannot fully explain, I decided to get off 1S72 and pick up 55006 on the following 2315 to Bradford. As Mighty **MELD** powered away into the Night with her Napier's roaring fiercely, the first twinges of regret set in. This regret was compounded the next day as I observed **MELD** arriving in York's platform 9 at the head of 1V93. Some you win and some you lose.

55004- On Saturday December 1st 1979, a gang of us were travelling down road behind **GORDON HIGHLANDER** on 1S12, as we left Peterborough, 55004 sat on the depot a few hours after an 18 month sojourn in Doncaster Works had finally ended. No 4 looked like a patchwork quilt with shiny blue paint covering the rust patches and faded blue paint just about everywhere else. However, she sat on a pair of new clean bogies, I had never seen a Deltic looking so peculiar, It was a captivating sight, Chris Short told me that he had sat in the cab the day before and many of the controls were rusty and the cab felt damp and lifeless. For the whole of that weekend every time I passed through Peterborough, I willed her to come off shed and work a train, sadly this never happened and I had to wait until January 2nd to enjoy my first ride behind **QUEENS OWN HIGHLANDER**.

55005- POWORY was another Deltic which always seemed to be about whenever I was and for this reason, I have several memories of this fine machine. In October 1978 whilst travelling back to Scotland after the Half Term holidays, our chosen train home was the 0900 Kings Cross to Edinburgh. I was delighted to find number 5 at the head of the train, and we enjoyed a superb run to Edinburgh. A year later and this time almost 20 hours in the Prince's company, Kings Cross to Edinburgh on 1S72 and then York and back on 1V93 and 1S27. Number 5 had only recently had her final classified light repair at Doncaster and was in a very clean external condition along with performing superbly.

55006- In my opinion the best of the fleet in terms of performance and availability, Number 6 never let me down and I can never remember hearing anyone have a wrong word to say about her. Similar to 55005 it has been very difficult to pick just one memory of FAFY. The memory chosen is a linked one from March 1980. Number 6 had just been released from works following a power unit change and was heading to Scotland on 1S72 which I happened to join at Darlington. As we headed north passed the DMU depot it quickly became apparent that No 6 was making the most awesome racket. The normal Napier sound was much louder and deeper with an underlying screaming sound from one of the power units. The sound had me mesmerised and sleep became impossibility as we bellowed our way through the Northumbrian countryside and over the border into Scotland. The next night I was with Ian Flynn at Waverley to watch the departure of 1E35 which 55006 was working to London. I remember saying to Ian wait until you hear the racket this is going to make. Sure enough as the train left Carlton tunnel the second engine must have cut in because even though we were still on platform 7, we could hear the locomotive powering away into the night for several minutes. I have heard other people say similar things about other Deltics over the years and often wonder if a rational explanation exists.

55007- Back to 1974 and Leeds City station. My Grandfather and I were spending a few hours watching the comings and goings when **PINZA** arrived with a very late running Kings Cross service. The locomotive was covered in oil all along one side as was much of the leading coach. I remember being invited into the warm cab by the friendly driver as the train was emptied and the shunter uncoupled the locomotive.

After running round the stock 55007 left on its return to London and covered the station throat in blue haze as it accelerated round onto the viaduct on the now closed Geldard Road route. I am unsure as to the cause of the oil leak or indeed if **PINZA** failed as a consequence, however the noise, oil and vibration only further cemented my love of the 55.

55008- July 1981 and the last summer in the life of our beloved Deltics. Steve MacFarlane, Paul Gildersleve and I found ourselves at Kings Cross awaiting a trip north with 55008 on the 1403 to York. For some reason that day the train was formed of 90 mph vacuum braked stock, instead of the usual 100mph mark two's. We stood on platform 6 admiring number 8 prior to departure. It was a hot sultry summer's day and 55008 looked a picture of power with her black domino headcode and nose ends covered in millions of dead flies, her rippled, and bulging work stained flanks exaggerated in the light and shade of a perfect summer's afternoon. I noticed the driver happened to be reading a railway magazine; I commented to this fact to Steve and said we may be in for a good run. This was an understatement as what took place next was beyond our wildest dreams. The ageing vacuum braked stock was hustled, bounced and rattled northwards at speeds of up to 112mph as every ounce of power was wrung out of 55008's Napier engines. Not content with this north bound show of brute power, the same driver put in an even better display on the return to Kings Cross with 1A31. Sweeping down Stoke, mile after mile at 110 mph, the sheer theatre of it all had us in raptures none more so than Mr Hillingdon who's stopwatch hand was whizzing round every quarter of a mile as number 8 swept southwards with a majesty no other class of locomotive could ever muster.

55009- Some of my best memories of **ALYCIDON** are from the preservation era and not her B.R career. Whilst she became one of my highest mileage Deltics, trips behind Alice always seemed mundane and lacking the excitement of some of her stable mates. In many respects she did all of the things Deltics were purchased for, which was to go about daily life in a no fuss, no nonsense way earning revenue for the company. In my opinion number 9 really came into the limelight with the launch of her second mainline career in 1999. Who can forget the run to York and back on May 22nd or the trip to Stirling a few months later and not be impressed with the pedigree of this re-born thorough bread. This all culminated with the Deltic Freedom of Scotland tour in 2003 and a chance to sample Deltic power over all of my former Highland stomping grounds. Even my mother was moved to stand in her garden and listen to **ALYCIDON** powering up Conon Bank almost 3 miles away.

55010- The second of June 1979 was not my first trip with number 10, but it was certainly the most memorable. I was heading back to Scotland after spending the half term holidays (my final ones as I left school 5 weeks later) chasing Deltics. I was just about to struggle to find a seat on a very busy 2000 to Aberdeen for a night's haulage with **PINZA**, when I heard the drone of another Deltic approaching the station. 55010 buffered up to the stock of the 2015 to Edinburgh. Therefore 1S60 was only taken to Peterborough as a dose of number 10 really appealed. 1S66 was a more sociable train for sleep, due to the propensity for the Aberdeen train to carry large numbers of oil workers ready for early morning flights out to the rigs. I slept most of the way to Newcastle and woke to the sight of **PINZA** in the adjacent platform ready to head over the Tyne Valley with 1S60. After running round the stock number 10 was soon ready to follow west. More sleep took place between Newcastle and Carlisle ahead of the main event which was the climb of Beattock Bank. At Carlisle upon looking out of the quarter light window of my compartment; I observed that the conductor driver was at the controls, which I would suggest was the exception and not the norm on these trains. Once clear of the station area and its 20 mph speed restriction, the power handle was pulled wide open and the night was filled with number 10's unleashed fury. As the second engine cut in lumps of hot burning carbon poured out of one of the exhausts to such an extent that I had to sit down and close the window, this continued for some time and a veritable meteorite storm passed the window. After passing Kingmoor Yard, I went to wash my face in the hope of removing some of the oil and muck. To my amazement I discovered the seat in the compartment behind me was smouldering and on the verge of catching fire, a huge hole had already appeared in the cushion. I ran to the end of the coach to grab one of the water fire extinguishers to be met by the guard running towards me extinguisher in hand. With disaster averted we could only speculate that the pyrotechnics from number 10 had resulted in a piece of something hot coming in through the window and landing on the seat, an adventure and a further insight into Deltic mythology.

55011 – Considering the number of runs I have had with this fine machine my choice for number 11 may be considered surprising to some. On October 4th 1981, I enjoyed my last run with this Deltic. A group of us ended up in Newcastle one evening with a view to heading south for Kings Cross. Class 55 haulage, particularly on a Saturday night was now becoming much harder to find and the nights of endless overnights had gone forever. I cannot remember the names of everyone who was there, but I recollect Phillip Wormald or Barney Rubble (cockney rhyming slang for trouble) as we knew him, come back with the news that 55011 was allocated to and would be working 1A40 through to London. Number 11 had been on one engine for some days by this time but had continued to put in some sterling work on overnight and secondary passenger trains. Powering up the Team Valley and out into the night number 11 sounded magnificent and I felt genuine emotion that once again she had appeared when all seemed lost. We arrived in London at some ungodly hour on Sunday morning and stood around for some time admiring the worked stained Deltic. For me intuition was telling me that this was almost certainly my last trip with her. I was not out again until the end of November by which time her remaining engine would have almost certainly succumbed to failure. This indeed happened some time later in of all places Liverpool. A fitting memory for a Deltic which was always there and had never let me down in over 6000 miles.

55012- Despite several Anglo-Scottish trips during the heyday of this machine, my choice for **CREPELLO** involves a trip from Peterborough to London not long before receiving white cabs. She was hauling a scratch set of coaches on a York to Kings Cross job and I was in the leading BSO which unusually for a south bound train placed me immediately behind the locomotive. With the brake van and guards compartment between the seating area and the rest of the train other passengers must have been deterred from walking through as I had all 30 odd seats to myself. As we powered south the low sun made a perfect silhouette of **CREPELLO** in shadow on the down fast line. The outline was so perfect as to be able to pick out the shape of the air horns and even the small air pipes from which they were supplied with compressed air. Every time power was applied the silhouette grew to reflect both locomotive and exhaust. This was another one of those magical and much missed experiences which I had all to myself.

55013- I have been blessed with many fine runs down the years, from Anglo Scottish express trains, to overnights and locals with this iconic Deltic. My choice in her memory involves a run on the down *Hull Executive* in the summer of 1979. The run from Kings Cross to Hitchin was dogged by delay and an apparent problem with the locomotive or coaching stock. We finally came to a stand on the down main somewhere south of Hitchin and both driver and guard walked down the cess side releasing the brakes on each of the 8 mark 2d coaches. After around 20 minutes delay we were off again. With a wound up driver and time to make up **THE BLACK WATCH** went on the rampage with some fine running. Standing in the leading vestibule, I watched through the small coach end window the bright yellow snout pitching and swaying as speed increased, I was mesmerised by the awesome display of power taking place a few feet ahead of me. Whatever the root cause of the delay ultimately turned out to be no loss of time could possibly have been booked to 55013 or the crew. Alighting at Retford for 1A31 we stood on the platform and drank in the magnificence of our steed. In the confined space between the throbbing Deltic and the white wooden fence protecting the fast lines the awesome power of Napier's made your whole torso vibrate. With a hiss of releasing air brake and a long parp on the horn **THE BLACK WATCH** departed north for Doncaster and its ultimate destination of Hull.

55014- Whenever I was out and about number 14 more often than not wasn't. Exams at home depot or main works visits to Doncaster always seem to coincide with any prolonged period that I have arranged on the ECML. In an attempt to mitigate this whenever I got on board a 'Super Duke' hauled train, I would stick with it for as long as reasonably sensible to help rack up the miles. This strategy was employed right until the end and my last trip with her in October 1981. With the Deltics now in their 11th hour, I was delighted to find 55014 back down onto the Sundays 1005 Kings Cross to York service. A trip to York and back via the Joint Line was the only game in town on what I remember as an unseasonably warm sunny day. The trip itself was nothing special, not unlike the previous 19 runs behind 55014. On the return quite a crowd of us gathered to enjoy a dose of number 14 and the last ever daytime diversion via Lincoln. The thing that really made the trip so memorable is on the return trip just north of Werrington Junction, I became a member of the exclusive 100k club as my Deltic mileage crossed the 100 000 mark. The irony was not lost on me that this milestone was achieved behind my lowest mileage 55 of all those who made it into 1981.

55015- I have so many wonderful memories of **TULYAR** all of which apart from the last day are from the 1977-79 period. Following her final classified overhaul she became just another Deltic and seemed to have lost some of the charismatic charm of the past. During the Christmas holidays of 1978, I spent every spare minute at Kings Cross, or on the odd trip to Peterborough. The only rule my family imposed upon me was as a 14 year old, I could not leave the station and needed to catch the 1624 Waterloo to Epsom home to my aunt's house in the evening. To ensure compliance with this rule, I watched the departure of the *Leeds Executive* before heading onto the underground and Waterloo. The last

Saturday before Christmas was cold and a freezing fog had set in as I stood on platform 2 awaiting the arrival of the Deltic for the 1545 Leeds. It had been a good day Deltic wise and it was with no surprise when **TULYAR** which had worked up on the 0800 from Edinburgh backed down onto the 8 coaches to form this service. With both engines running and the locomotive under the train shed roof the air was filled with the cacophony of sound from 3300 horses waiting to be unleashed. As I stood taking it all in, the drivers sliding door opened and to my surprise an invite was made for me to come aboard. Climbing into the narrow passageway linking the engine room and cab, I could feel the welcoming warmth of the cab along with the smell of leather, oil and years of hard work. It was a feeling that I would get to know well over the coming years. I have vivid memories of seeing the little row of fault lights on the side of the control cubicle along with the weight of the leather sound deadening curtain as I pushed it aside to get into the cramped cab. The friendly Kings Cross driver pointed towards the secondments seat and requested I make myself comfortable. In the 5 minutes or so that I spent looking out over the bonnet and into the gloom of the station throat memories and emotions became engrained in me which have lasted until the present day. All too soon I had to return to the platform and watch number 15 depart in the customary cloud of blue exhaust. As the taillight disappeared into Gasworks Tunnel, I walked towards the underground with a grin of satisfaction on my face.

55016- A freezing snowbound December 29th 1978. The day had not been a productive one from a Deltic perspective. I had just alighted from a 55006 hauled 1411 York to Kings Cross at a bitterly cold Doncaster. With not much happening in the station area it was time to walk round to the back of Doncaster Works with a view to seeing if the absence of Deltics had anything to do with what it may contain within its walls. Walking over Hexthorpe Road bridge darkness was already setting in, to help intensify the feeling of mid-winter gloom. Glancing southwards, the 'eyes' of a Deltic came into view as the 1300 Kings Cross to Edinburgh slowed for its booked stop. The Deltic at the head of the train was none other than **GORDON HIGHLANDER** a locomotive that I had previously thought ensconced inside Doncaster Works awaiting power units. The Haymarket stalwart was utterly filthy and the low levels of ambient light, made its head code eyes glare with a dark malevolence as it mumbled underneath me into the station. I stood there feeling well and truly bowled out. I had completely forgotten about 1S28 having a Doncaster stop and would have paid a high price to ride north with 55016, on what was one of its rare forays out of works. Sadly it was not to be and a few days later a power unit failure forced another long sojourn in works and it would be nearly 10 months before we would meet up again at Grantham.

55017- Another Deltic which in my view fell into the average performer but always around category. Despite over 30 runs to choose from my choice is not of a run behind the DLI but a memory of seeing her in action. In the Easter Holidays of 1977 my family and I were driving from Scotland to North Yorkshire when we stopped for a break at a truck stop near Grantshouse in the Scottish Borders. As soon as the car door was opened the sound of an approaching Deltic could be heard from the South. 55017 and a long rake of blue and grey air conditioned coaches came sweeping majestically into view round the reverse curves at Houndwood. With a blast on the horn **THE DURHAM LIGHT INFANTRY** swept passed, with the sun shining off the bright yellow nose heading the 1100 from Kings Cross to Edinburgh. The sound of the receding 55 could be heard until the DLI plunged into confines of Penmanshiel tunnel. The whole event had lasted no more than perhaps 2 minutes, the memory however will last a lifetime.

55018- In May 1977, I was spending an afternoon in the warm spring sunshine at Northallerton station watching Deltics at speed. It had been an excellent day with many of these fine machines doing the job for which they were built, hammering along the ECML metals with a dozen or so coaches in tow. With all our sandwiches eaten and drink bottles empty, It was getting to that time of day when we began to think about packing up our things and catching the bus back to Richmond. However our deliberations were interrupted, by the singing of rails and the sound of a Deltic approaching at speed from the south. In the blink of an eye **BALLYMOSS** was upon us as she swept through the station with a flash of yellow snout, a demented untamed bellow along with the following rush of warm air as the crew looked out of the narrow windscreen possibly taking in for a few seconds the scene of unrestrained joy on the opposite platform. Our notebooks and jumpers fluttered on the platform beside us as the coaches of the down *Aberdonian* tore passed and added to the general disturbance of the peace. As tranquillity returned to the sleepy North Yorkshire station we stood and watched the tail lamp of the train disappearing into the distance as a rampaging **BALLYMOSS** headed for Newcastle and beyond. Within a few weeks The MOSS would be called to works for a final intermediate overhaul along with the removal of the non-standard miniature white head eyes. This was my last memory of her in this condition, and is another event which seems only yesterday.

55019- The Easter Holidays in 1974 coincided with my 11th birthday. Snow in the Highlands had made our class 24/26 hauled train from Inverness almost an hour late upon arrival at Edinburgh. By the time we joined it the Queue for the *Aberdonian* was immense and intending passengers were being directed to a relief service on platform 10 hauled by 47 something or other. My mother was considering a walk from platform 19 to 10, when the drone of an approaching Deltic signified 1E14 was to enjoy its booked power southwards to Kings Cross, 55019 drew to a halt in the east end loop or platform 1/2 as it is now better known. A Deltic on my birthday was too good to miss and after much nagging an agreement was reached, just as the 47 spluttered past with the inwards arrival from Aberdeen. Despite all the ensuring pandemonium we found a pair of empty seats in the rear coach and settled down for the 205 mile trip to York. **ROYAL HIGHLAND FUSILIER** made light work of the heavy train as we headed south into much more clement weather. Speeding over the Vale of York with consummate ease, I have vivid memories of how green the grass looked in the rich fertile fields along with the white horse and hills to the east, all very much in contrast to what we had left behind. All too soon it was over and we arrived in platform 8 at York for an onwards connection to Leeds.

55020- My most poignant memory of **NIMBUS** involves nothing more than a photograph. In February 1980 I was travelling south behind **CREPELLO** when I first heard news of the demise of this exceptional and much loved machine. Paul Gash was passing round a picture of number 20 with one cab removed, surrounded by gas bottles and the control cubicle exposed to the elements for all to see (this picture can be found on page 3 of the book Last days of the Deltics) Obviously I had never seen such an image before and if I had any doubt that the end of the Deltic reign was imminent then this picture graphically reminded me that the axe man had arrived and was willing to do his duty. Even now over 40 years later the image of **NIMBUS** dethroned, shorn of dignity, days away from oblivion provoke emotion in me; the beginning of the end had begun. As a 17 year old, life still seemed full of endless possibility and optimism, that picture robbed me of some of that innocence and was a hard lesson in valuing what you have, because it will not be around forever. Many much worse images of the butchering of Deltic carcasses exist, however there is something about that black and white photograph that resonates deep within my soul, no other image will ever recreate such a feeling of impending doom.

55021- I have so many happy memories of The ASH going back to my first sighting of her at York in 1969 right through to my last encounter with her on December 31st 1981. She was a solid performer and I don't ever remember a sub-standard or one engine run with her. As Pete Wilcox and I often used to joke she fitted the bill of an engine with big shiny nameplates and crests perfectly. The encounter which best summaries this fine locomotive took place at Darlington in the summer of 1977. I had just watched **ST PADDY** depart north with the *Silver Jubilee* when almost at once the sound of another approaching Deltic could be heard from the south, as 55021 appeared heading a motley collection of parcels vans and came to a halt by the ticket barrier on platform 4. The train, as I found out in later years was the 6E05 Oxford to Newcastle vans. 55021 was being used vice a much lesser powered locomotive as she was operating on one engine and bound for Haymarket and repairs. During the 5/6 minute dwell time, I admired the sleek powerful lines of the Deltic from every possible conceivable angle. Even with only one engine operating the ASH sounded amazing under the station canopy and the curve of the roof line quickly filled with exhaust. The size and shape of the locomotives crest captivated me and really brought the flank of the locomotive to life in a way that didn't quite work for me once the crests had been removed.

55022- One memory for stands head and shoulders above the rest for **ROYAL SCOTS GREY** and that was her last run in BR ownership from Edinburgh to Kings Cross on January 2nd 1982, the actual events of which have been well documented many times before. The day started like any other, just a group of lads enjoying a day out on the ECML. Much of the north bound trip was spent helping in the Buffet car with the steward Colin making sandwiches and pouring hot drinks. I can't say that I was all that emotional to be frank. I had drifted away from Deltic bashing since my last rover at the end of October and my rehabilitation into a normal teenage life was well underway. It was only on the return as **ROYAL SCOTS GREY** powered southwards it slowly began to dawn on me that it really was all over and many people that I shared a common interest with, would be saying farewell to each other for the last time a few hours later. The crowds grew at every station we passed through, and one could not help but begin to be burdened by the huge sense of occasion. After Stevenage we were checked by signals, before RSG was wound up for her last hurrah. The cold frosty air was filled with the sound of hard working Napier's as we accelerated back up to line speed. At 2002 hours a huge part of my life ended and a void was created which took many years to completely fill. Many of us adjourned to the Malt and Hops (now a wine bar) for a farewell drink before dispersing to various parts of the United Kingdom and home. Harry Hall and I shared a compartment on 1S72; my first and last non Deltic hauled run to Edinburgh on this train. At Retford, 55022 silently passed us on the down main as she headed for York and withdrawal. That was when the emotion hit me like a sledge hammer, it really was all over and life would never be the same again.

After 20 years' service and around 3 million miles in traffic we see 55010 being prematurely reduced to scrap metal in May 1982. The locomotive had only received an expensive classified overhaul in October 1980 and had years of useful service left to give. However as Eastern and BR Management had an anything but Deltics mind set (this has subsequently been confirmed to me by someone on the inside at the time) then logic went out of the window and the original 1984 withdrawal plan was brought forwards to 1981 with no real thought as to how the duel braked and ETH loco plan was to be resourced going forwards.

Printed in Great Britain
by Amazon